Quadrille

Photographs by David Loftus

Nathan
Outlaw's
British
Seafood

To Rachel, my wife and best friend,
for everything you have done to
support my dream, and to my two
beautiful children Jacob and Jessica.
I love you more than anything in the world.

Foreword by Rick Stein

If Nathan Outlaw was the most aggressive and arrogant of chefs I would still have lots of time for him because he loves his fish. For me, almost the best bits of *Nathan Outlaw's British Seafood* are the descriptions of all the Cornish fish and shellfish he uses in the book – vivid descriptions of colour, texture and taste, always with a personal observation from his experience of cooking some of the best seafood in the world. But, in fact, Nathan is an utterly charming, self-effacing man who seems somewhat perplexed about the fact that he has two Michelin stars because he says it's only simple cooking.

Isn't it amazing how we see ourselves as opposed to the way others see us? To me, yes, the cooking is simple in that he uses mostly local ingredients and easy techniques, but to get there you have to have a wealth of experience. Experience, which I'm glad to say, included a long spell in my own kitchen right at the beginning of his career. I remember what a pleasure it was to have this large youth working in my kitchen, who was absolutely unequivocally going to be a chef. His father is a chef and Nathan will always be a chef.

Nathan understood the simple way that I like to cook and he was an enormously valuable asset in my kitchen. So, when he then went off to work in a number of restaurants with much more elaborate cooking, I rather stupidly felt irritated that such a good cook should go off and work in restaurants with a style of cooking that I find hard to take to my heart. But, of course, he had to do that. He had to work out where his own style lay and that must involve trying a whole raft of different cooking approaches. This book means a lot to me, because it's quite clear that Nathan's come of age and I feel personally proud that he hasn't forgotten some of the things that working for me taught him.

The book is a joy, I love the honesty of it. The recipes are appetising and easy and, above all, do justice to the great seafood which both Nathan and I are lucky enough to have delivered to our restaurants on a daily basis. I also think that in David Loftus he has found the perfect photographer to make his dishes come alive on the page.

Introduction

British seafood is my passion. I love everything about it: the catching, the prepping, the cooking and the happy faces in my restaurants when people are eating it. Fish and the sea fascinate me to the point of sitting in a daze watching the waves roll in, or searching around rock pools for any crab that might have got stuck behind when the tide has gone out. It can be anything that excites me about cooking and eating seafood – from the simplest of grilled fish dishes to the challenge of eating a whole crab, or the complexity of a great seafood stew.

I became interested in cooking when I was very young, inspired by my Mum, who is a great home cook, and my Dad, who is a chef and a very good one at that. Helping out in his kitchens was enough to make me realise that I wanted to be a chef. After my training, and working in London for a couple of years, I moved to Cornwall to work for Rick Stein at his Seafood Restaurant in Padstow. This is where I started to get really excited about seafood. I was handling the freshest and finest fish and shellfish I had ever seen: sea bass still alive in the sink, lobsters that would fight you as you put them in the tank, more varieties of oyster than I ever knew existed... I learnt everything about prepping and cooking British seafood and I began to appreciate that the key to great dishes is simplicity. I couldn't wait to have my own restaurant.

I was 25 when The Black Pig opened in Rock in 2003, and I was thrilled when it was awarded a Michelin star 8 months later. I moved to Fowey in 2007 to launch Restaurant Nathan Outlaw, but I knew I would return to Rock one day. Sure enough, in 2010 we relocated to St Enodoc Hotel in Rock, where I cook in my fine dining restaurant, now with two Michelin stars. My more casual family-style Seafood and Grill restaurant is also at the hotel.

I have written this book to convey my style of British seafood cookery. My approach is essentially simple and allows the ingredients and flavours to speak for themselves. I believe that this is the way to cook great seafood dishes. Sustainability is very important to me and, at the time of writing these recipes, all of the fish and shellfish I have used is sustainable, as it should be.

The book is divided into sections, covering each of the fish and shellfish available in the UK that I enjoy to eat and cook. I've given you information about the individual species, including advice on the best time of the year to eat them. I've also guided you towards the best cooking techniques to use and shown you how you can mix and match seafood with different sauces, dressings and accompaniments to create your own bespoke dishes. This is very much the way I cook.

For each fish and shellfish, I've given you two or three recipes. Some are simple and quick, the kind I cook at home. Others are sharing family-style dishes that I make when we have family and friends around for a leisurely lunch or dinner. I've also included signature dishes from my restaurant, the sort that you might cook for a dinner party. Please don't feel you have to follow any of my recipes to the letter, I just want to encourage you to cook and enjoy seafood. Feel free to chop and change flavouring ingredients, cooking techniques and sauces as you please. I hope you'll find plenty to inspire you and that this becomes the first book you grab whenever you buy seafood.

Buying & choosing seafood

It goes without saying that for any of the recipes you need fresh seafood. The best way of getting this is to build up a relationship with a fishmonger, or the staff at a good fish counter in a local supermarket, or, if you're lucky enough to be living near the coast, with a generous fisherman.

Fish
The quality of fresh fish is very much dependent on the way it's been transported. You usually find that bad fish comes from poor handling, a long journey or a dodgy fridge along the way…

When choosing fish, check that the eyes are bright and clear. Sunken and cloudy eyes indicate that the fish is old. Obviously, have a good sniff! The fish should smell of the sea – ozoney and seasidey – rather than unpleasant and with a strong fishy smell.

Flat fish should be firm and covered with a healthy sea slime – this is natural and a good sign of freshness. With oily fish like herring, mackerel and sardines, it's important that the skin colour is vivid and vibrant, almost like petrol on water. And finally, when buying fish that should have scales, make sure they are still in place.

Ideally, you won't be thinking about storing fish, as it is really best eaten within 24 hours of buying. However, if you have to store it, this is what you need to remember. Fish like to be stored between 0 and 2°C, covered with a layer of fresh ice. As soon as you get your fish home, wrap it in a damp cloth and put it in the coldest part of your fridge; don't let it sit in water. Stored in the correct manner, most fish will keep on the bone for several days, possibly longer. If you live some distance from your fishmonger, take a cool bag with you to ensure that it makes its way home in good condition.

If you have an abundance of fish, it's best to freeze it as soon as possible. The ideal way to do this is to freeze it off the bone, dried off and wrapped tightly in cling film. Fish will be fine in your freezer for up to 2 months as long as it is well wrapped.

Shellfish
When buying shellfish to cook, with the exception of scallops, they should always be live. All shellfish should be clean and smell of the sea.

Clams, cockles, mussels and oysters should be tightly shut, or ready to close when tapped. These molluscs all filter seawater through their bodies, so it is important to know where they have come from, and that they have been treated safely to eliminate any harmful bacteria.

In an ideal world, you would buy live scallops too, but these are not always available. More often than not, scallops are sold already cut from the shell. If you do buy live scallops, make sure they are tightly closed or will close up when touched. When buying cut scallops, make sure they are firm, smell ozoney and sweet, and have not been soaked.

When buying uncooked lobsters and crabs, again, check that they are alive. Also make sure there are no visible bubbles coming from their mouths, which is a sign of stress and will affect the eating quality of the meat.

With lobsters, look for long antennae. Short antennae suggest that the lobster has been stored for a long time and has begun to eat itself, or has been eaten by others.

All cephalopods – cuttlefish, squid and octopus – are best eaten within 2 days of being caught. However, all varieties freeze well, so it's fine to buy them frozen if this is your only option. When buying, look for a healthy slime and no sign of pinkness, which indicates that the cephalopod has seen better days. As with fish, make sure the eyes are bright and that the cuttlefish, squid or octopus are intact, which is likely to mean they have been transported and stored carefully.

Cooking techniques

Roasting
I roast whole fish and tranches on the bone. Heat your oven to 200°C/Gas 6. Before you start cooking the fish, make sure you have everything else you are cooking ready. Take a baking tray that is big enough to accommodate all the fish with space around so that it isn't packed too tightly together. Lightly oil or butter and season the tray with salt and pepper. Oil the fish or dot it with butter, season, then place it on the tray. If you are worried about your fish sticking, lay it on a piece of non-stick baking paper or silicone paper on the tray before oiling and seasoning.

Slide the baking tray into the oven and bake the fish until it is just cooked – the flesh should flake perfectly. Halfway through cooking, baste your fish with the cooking juices from the tray to keep it moist. Obviously the size and thickness of the fish determines the cooking time. Smaller fish like red mullet will cook in 8–10 minutes, while a sea bass will take 20–30 minutes. For really big

fish, turn the oven down to 180°C/Gas 4 after 10 minutes or so, or the outside of the fish will singe. When your fish is cooked, don't throw the juices away – they are full of flavour and can be spooned over the fish before serving.

Grilling or char-grilling
Small to medium whole fish and fillets are suitable for grilling. First, heat your grill. The heat level will depend on the size and thickness of the fish. For instance, a mackerel is fine under a hot grill but a sea bass needs a medium grill, otherwise it will scorch on the outside before it is cooked through. Most fish need a medium or medium-high heat. Oil and season the grill tray and the fish. When you are grilling any fish you need to keep a close eye on it. The intensity of grills varies enormously and there is nothing worse than overcooked, dry fish!

If you are barbecuing or char-grilling, put the bigger fish on the outer, cooler part of the griddle, but make sure it is not too cool or the skin will stick.

Steaming
This is a good way to cook delicate fillets and pieces of skate or ray. Place the fish on buttered non-stick baking paper or silicone paper, or even a butter paper, to stop the fish sticking to the steamer. I like to add seaweed or citrus peel to the simmering water to impart a subtle flavour. The cooking time will vary according to the size and thickness of the fish. As a guide, a medium-thick 200g piece of fish will take about 6 minutes.

Clams, cockles and mussels are steamed too – in a tightly closed large saucepan with a little liquid to create the steam.

Pan-frying
Anyone who is serious about fish cookery needs a decent non-stick frying pan, preferably one that is ovenproof. Pan-frying is the technique I use more than any other and I sometimes start by frying the fish in the pan on the hob, then finish off the cooking in the oven.

First, make sure your fish fillets are dry by placing them on some kitchen paper or a clean J cloth. Heat your pan over a medium heat, never a high heat. If you put very fresh fish into a very hot pan it will curl up and the skin

INTRODUCTION

will split. Fish fried over a high heat will overcook on the outside before it is cooked in the middle, so always use a medium heat.

When your pan is hot, add the oil. I like to use rapeseed or light olive oil. Place your fish carefully, skin side or presentation side down, in the pan. Season the side uppermost with salt and pepper and cook for 2–3 minutes or until the edges of the fish begin to go golden. At this stage, depending on the size of fish, you have two options. You can flip the fish over and fry it for another 2–3 minutes until ready to serve. Or, if it's a bigger piece of fish, you can slide the pan into a hot oven at 200°C/ Gas 6 and cook for another 3 minutes or until ready. In this case, do not flip it; keep it skin side down so you get a lovely crispy skin. Remember with pan-frying that the residual heat of the pan will finish off the cooking. So cook your fish a little bit under and leave it to finish off in the pan while you put the rest of your dish together.

Deep-frying
I deep-fry pieces of fish, such as goujons and fillets of white fish like monkfish, plaice and turbot, as well as squid rings and Pacific oysters, first coating them in breadcrumbs or a light batter to protect them. I use sunflower or light rapeseed oil and heat it to 180°C, no hotter. The cooking time depends on the size of the pieces, but in general, most fish and shellfish will take 3–5 minutes.

If you have a deep-fryer with a basket, put the basket into the oil before you add the fish, otherwise the pieces of fish will stick to the basket. When dealing with larger fillets of fish, hold them firmly by the tail and lower them into the oil one at a time, allowing the tail to fall away from you, rather than towards you, as the hot oil will surge and may spit and burn your hand.

When the fish is cooked, drain it on kitchen paper and give it a light seasoning of salt; this helps to keep it crispy by drawing out the excess oil.

Flat
white
fish

Brill

This is the fish that would always be picked second in the playground after turbot, but in my opinion brill is as good as turbot, if not better. In fact the two fish are so close in the way they live that they have been known to interbreed. Brill is at its finest between October and March when it's in season. The fish spawn in the spring and summer so this is the time to avoid them. Before spawning, female fish over 3 years old will contain a huge amount of roe and are not at their best for eating, so avoid these.

Brill live at the bottom of the ocean and can be found in the Atlantic, Mediterranean and Baltic Sea. The younger fish feed on plankton and then move onto crustaceans and small fish. Try to avoid brill from the North Sea as it can be an immature by-catch from beam trawlers. Your fishmonger should be able to tell you where it is from.

Brill isn't the cheapest of fish, but at its best you get what you pay for. Brill grows to about 75cm and can weigh in at up to 3kg. Firm, thick, boneless fillets from bigger fish benefit from poaching or roasting, while those cut from smaller fish are better suited to a gentle grilling or coating in light breadcrumbs and frying. Personally, I like a more versatile 2kg fish, which can be cooked using any of these methods. The texture of brill is not as firm as turbot, but firmer than Dover sole. It is a fish that can handle both delicate and strong flavours, working equally well with a light cream sauce or a full-bodied red wine sauce. The skin isn't pleasant to eat though, so I'd recommend that you remove it before cooking or simply don't eat it. On the other hand, the bones and head from this fish make a superior stock for a fine sauce, so always use them. My favourite way to cook and eat brill is on the bone – the texture, juices and flavour seem so much more fantastic as you pull the flesh away from the bone.

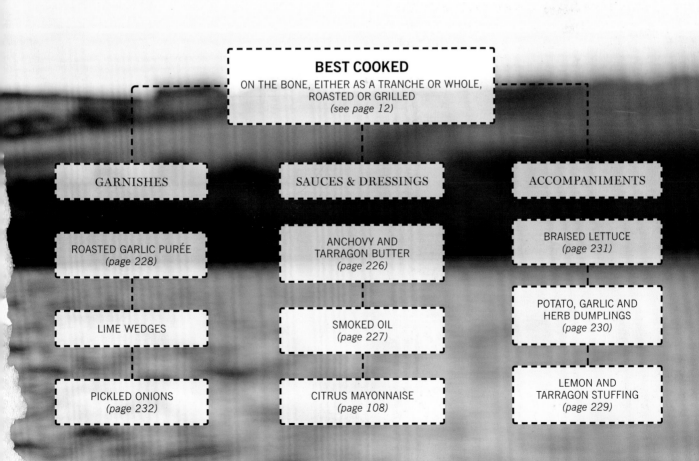

BEST COOKED
ON THE BONE, EITHER AS A TRANCHE OR WHOLE,
ROASTED OR GRILLED
(see page 12)

GARNISHES

ROASTED GARLIC PURÉE
(page 228)

LIME WEDGES

PICKLED ONIONS
(page 232)

SAUCES & DRESSINGS

ANCHOVY AND
TARRAGON BUTTER
(page 226)

SMOKED OIL
(page 227)

CITRUS MAYONNAISE
(page 108)

ACCOMPANIMENTS

BRAISED LETTUCE
(page 231)

POTATO, GARLIC AND
HERB DUMPLINGS
(page 230)

LEMON AND
TARRAGON STUFFING
(page 229)

Brill with brown shrimps and griddled leeks in a mustard dressing

The flavour of brill combined with mustard, leeks and shrimps is one of my favourites. It is so good! If you can't get brown shrimps, then use prawns instead. When I'm serving this dish as a light lunch, I like to have a dressed salad and a bowl of minted new potatoes on the side.

Serves 4 as a starter or light lunch

4 filleted brill portions, about 150g each, skinned and trimmed

olive oil for cooking

20 baby leeks or 4 medium leeks, trimmed, washed and halved

Cornish sea salt

To finish

4–5 tbsp English mustard dressing (page 224)

100g cooked brown shrimps

3 tsp chopped chives

Heat your oven to 220°C/Gas 7, ready to cook the fish.

For the leeks, heat up a griddle pan over a high heat, if you have one, or heat your grill. Oil the pan or, if grilling, brush the leeks with olive oil. Cook the halved leeks on the griddle pan or under the grill for 1 minute on each side for baby leeks, 2 minutes each side for normal leeks. Season with salt and remove to a warm plate; keep warm.

Heat a large ovenproof non-stick frying pan over a medium heat and add a little olive oil. When the oil is hot, add the fish to the pan, skinned side up (ie presentation side down). Cook for about 2 minutes until the underside starts to turn golden, then place the pan in the oven for 3 minutes. Remove from the oven and carefully flip the fish over. Leave the fish in the pan while you assemble the dish; it will finish cooking in the residual heat.

Warm the mustard dressing in a small pan, but don't let it become too hot. Divide most of the leeks between 4 warmed plates, lay the fish over them and arrange the rest of the leeks on top. Toss the brown shrimps and chives with the dressing and spoon over and around the fish. Serve immediately.

Brill with roasted root vegetables and red wine sauce

This dish, from my Seafood and Grill restaurant, looks amazing and flies out of the kitchen door when we put it on the menu. Brill is at its best in the colder months; it goes without saying that root veg are at their best at this time too. I cook the fish on the bone for optimum flavour. A full-bodied red wine sauce takes the dish to a whole new level.

Serves 2

2 brill tranche portions, about 170g each (see page 242)

olive oil for cooking

5 garlic cloves (unpeeled)

2 thyme sprigs

50g unsalted butter, diced

Cornish sea salt and freshly ground black pepper

Roasted root vegetables

2 small or 1 large beetroot, cleaned

50ml white wine vinegar

2 carrots, peeled

2 parsnips, peeled

olive oil for cooking

1 red onion, peeled and cut into wedges, root end intact

3 garlic cloves, peeled and crushed

1 thyme sprig

50g unsalted butter

To serve

1 quantity red wine sauce (page 223)

1 garlic clove, peeled and finely chopped

2 tbsp chopped flat-leaf parsley

few thyme sprigs

Heat your oven to 220°C/Gas 7. For the roasted vegetables, place the beetroot in a small pan, add enough water to cover and the wine vinegar and bring to a simmer. Cook for about 15 minutes until a knife inserted into the beetroot meets with a little resistance, not until the beetroot are completely soft. Leave to cool in the water, then peel the beetroot with a small knife and cut roughly into 1cm thick rounds. Cut the carrots into similar sized rounds. Quarter the parsnips lengthways and cut out the woody core. Place the carrots in a pan of salted water and simmer for about 3 minutes until partially cooked, then add the parsnips and cook for a further 3 minutes. Drain the vegetables and allow to cool on a tray.

Drizzle some olive oil into a roasting tray large enough to hold all the vegetables. Add the red onion wedges, garlic and thyme and roast in the oven for 5 minutes. Add the par-cooked vegetables, season with salt and pepper and roast for 10 minutes.

Meanwhile, pat the brill dry with kitchen paper, place in a roasting tray and drizzle with some olive oil. Season with salt and pepper, add the unpeeled garlic cloves and thyme and place in the oven. Roast for 5 minutes, then dot the fish with the diced butter and return to the oven for 5 minutes. Baste the fish with the buttery juices and roast for a further 3 minutes. Baste the fish again and set aside in a warm place to rest for 5 minutes before serving.

While the fish is resting, bring the red wine sauce to the boil. Pour the cooking juices from the fish through a sieve into the sauce and bring back to a simmer. Add the chopped garlic and parsley and pour into a warm jug ready for serving.

Lay the brill portions on the roasted vegetables with the roasted garlic cloves and a few thyme sprigs. Serve at once, giving the sauce a stir before pouring it over the fish to re-distribute the garlic and parsley.

Cured brill with pistachio dressing, pink grapefruit and pickled chicory

This is my version of the Latin American dish, ceviche. Here I'm using brill, but it works equally well with scallops, turbot or salmon. Very fresh fish is crucial. The citrus juice marinade alters the texture of the fish, effectively taking out its rawness. The grapefruit and pistachio dressing works particularly well with the soft fish, and the crunchy, mellow, pickled chicory is the perfect complement.

Serves 4 as a starter or light lunch

600g brill fillet

Cure

1 fennel bulb, trimmed (tough outer layer removed)

juice of 2 pink grapefruit

2 small shallots, peeled and finely chopped

1 green chilli, deseeded and very thinly sliced

1 tsp caster sugar

pinch of smoked paprika

1 tbsp chopped fennel (herb)

2 tsp Cornish sea salt

Pickled chicory

2 heads of chicory, trimmed

100ml white wine

100ml white wine vinegar

100ml water

100ml caster sugar

Pistachio dressing

100g shelled, roasted and salted pistachios

about 50ml sunflower oil

To finish

100g watercress, washed and trimmed

100g rocket leaves, washed and trimmed

1 pink grapefruit, peel and pith removed, segmented

Slice the brill into 1cm pieces. For the cure, finely slice the fennel, using a mandolin if you have one. Mix all the ingredients for the cure together in a bowl, add the brill pieces and turn to coat. Cover and leave to marinate in a cool place for at least 2 hours and no longer than 5 hours.

For the pickled chicory, separate the leaves. Put the wine, wine vinegar and water into a small saucepan, add the sugar and a good pinch of salt and bring to the boil over a medium heat. Meanwhile, put the chicory leaves into a container that will hold them and the liquor. Pour the boiling liquid over the chicory, making sure it is submerged. Allow to cool before using. (The pickled chicory will keep in the fridge for up to a week.)

For the pistachio dressing, blitz the nuts in a food processor for 1 minute until finely chopped. Scrape down the nuts from the side of the bowl and add a little of the oil. Continue to blend, adding more oil as necessary, until the nut mixture is the consistency of a dressing. Set aside until ready to use. (The dressing will keep in the fridge for 2 weeks but should be brought to room temperature to serve.)

When you are ready to serve, drain the chicory and pat dry on kitchen paper. Taste the brill and adjust the seasoning if necessary. Drain the fish and fennel mixture, reserving the juice in a jug. Arrange the cured brill and fennel, watercress, rocket, pickled chicory and pink grapefruit segments on 4 serving plates. Dress with the pistachio dressing. Serve the reserved juice on the side for guests to add as they wish.

Dover sole

When people mention Dover sole, invariably I think 'grilled whole'. This is probably because its structure and texture – tightly packed flakes and juiciness – make it the perfect fish for cooking whole. Dover sole benefits from a few days of maturing in the fridge, as do other flat fish such as turbot and skate. If you attempt to cook a very fresh, stiff Dover sole you will find it tough and tasteless, not to mention the fact that it will probably curl up during cooking and split across the fillet, leaving you with an unattractive result. Dover sole fetches a very high price, so it's not a fish to ruin. Small Dover soles, called slip soles, are a great option as they are less expensive and a brace of these makes an excellent main course.

Dover sole doesn't come from Dover but it is named after the Kent port because in times past this was the most reliable route for the London fish market. Today Brixham is probably the busiest market for these fish. Dover soles are caught across the North Atlantic but those landed in the UK are considered to be the best in the world, and have been for centuries. In the early to mid 19th century the bigger the Dover sole on your table, the richer you were perceived to be. Unfortunately, back then, the flavour of these fine flat fish was also typically masked with lavish, heavy sauces, so the joy of eating such a wonderful fish was totally lost.

Dover soles feed at night, hiding themselves half buried in the sand waiting for little crustaceans and fish to cross their path. The breeding season is between April and June and the fish come inshore to spawn. You will find that the price of the fish comes down a bit at this time. You can still eat them, but they will yield much less flesh owing to the proportion of roe and I'd recommend avoiding them until the breeding season is over. Dover sole can get to a ripe old age of 40, but most are eaten at 5–6 years old. The 500g fish is the most popular size but personally I like the larger fish, which are ideal for sharing and great for an unusual Sunday lunch. The bigger 'doormats', as the fishermen call them, are available from February to April.

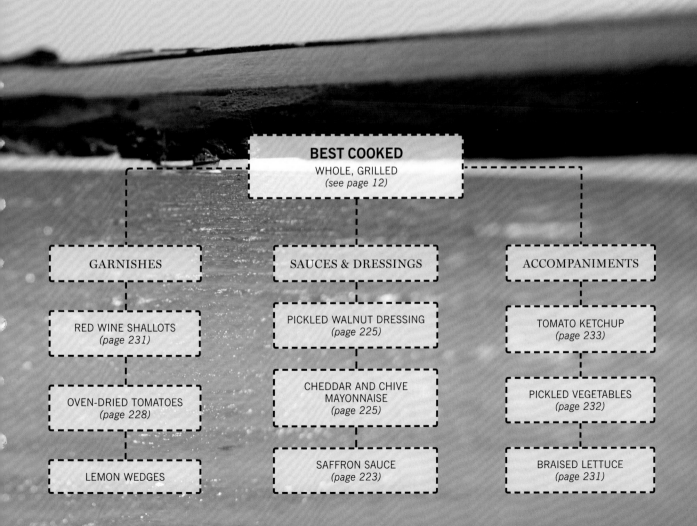

BEST COOKED
WHOLE, GRILLED
(see page 12)

GARNISHES	SAUCES & DRESSINGS	ACCOMPANIMENTS
RED WINE SHALLOTS *(page 231)*	PICKLED WALNUT DRESSING *(page 225)*	TOMATO KETCHUP *(page 233)*
OVEN-DRIED TOMATOES *(page 228)*	CHEDDAR AND CHIVE MAYONNAISE *(page 225)*	PICKLED VEGETABLES *(page 232)*
LEMON WEDGES	SAFFRON SAUCE *(page 223)*	BRAISED LETTUCE *(page 231)*

Dover sole fillets with lemon sauce and wild garlic dumplings

For this recipe I like to use the chunky fillets from bigger 'doormat' Dover sole, which are around when wild garlic is in season. It's a great pairing and the zingy lemon sauce brings the dish together a treat. When the scent of wild garlic, also known as ramsons, pervades the Cornish lanes, you know spring and warmer weather is on the way. You can use normal sized Dover sole, or indeed any other flat fish, here.

Serves 4

2 large Dover soles, 700–800g each, or 4 smaller 400–500g fish, filleted

rapeseed oil for cooking

20 purple sprouting or tenderstem broccoli stems

Cornish sea salt and freshly ground black pepper

Lemon sauce

1 egg yolk

finely grated zest and juice of 1 lemon

200ml light olive oil

50ml double cream

100ml roast fish stock (page 222)

To serve

wild garlic dumplings (page 230)

2 tsp shredded wild garlic (ramsons), optional

lemon oil (page 227) to drizzle

For the lemon sauce, whisk the egg yolk, lemon zest and juice together in a bowl for 1 minute and then slowly whisk in the olive oil, as for mayonnaise. Season with salt to taste and set aside.

Heat a splash of rapeseed oil in a large non-stick frying pan over a medium heat. Season the fish fillets and lay them in the pan, skin side down. Cook for 3 minutes, then turn and cook on the other side for 1 minute. Remove the pan from the heat and leave the fish to rest in the pan for a further 2 minutes.

While the fish is cooking, add the broccoli to a pan of boiling salted water and blanch for 3 minutes. At the same time, fry the dumplings, according to the recipe, in a little oil until golden.

Meanwhile, to finish the sauce, whisk in the cream, followed by the fish stock. Warm gently over a medium heat; do not allow to boil, or it will curdle. If the sauce is too thick, add a little more fish stock. Taste and season with a little more salt if required.

Drain the broccoli as soon as it is ready. Share it equally between 4 warmed plates and spoon on some of the lemon sauce. Place the fish on top, scatter over the shredded wild garlic, if using, and add the wild garlic dumplings. Drizzle with lemon oil. Serve at once, with the rest of the lemon sauce in a jug on the side.

Steamed Dover sole with pickled grape, roast garlic and parsley dressing

The smaller Dover sole fillets or even slip soles are best for this dish. Steaming them in a little wine and stock produces a small amount of tasty fish essence to add to the dressing. The pickled grapes are a lovely addition – my twist on the classic sole véronique. For a perfect lunch, serve this dish with a bowl of hot new potatoes and a simple salad of dressed peppery leaves, such as rocket or watercress.

Serves 4 as a starter or light lunch

4 Dover soles, 350–400g each, filleted and skinned

50g unsalted butter

1 shallot, peeled and chopped

50ml roast fish stock (page 222)

50ml white wine

Cornish sea salt and freshly ground black pepper

Dressing

20 pickled grapes (page 232)

2 tsp roasted garlic purée (page 228)

30ml good-quality white wine or champagne vinegar

150ml extra virgin olive oil

4 tsp chopped parsley

To finish

4 roasted garlic cloves (page 228)

For the dressing, slice the pickled grapes. Whisk the roasted garlic purée and wine vinegar together in a bowl and then gradually whisk in the extra virgin olive oil. Add the chopped parsley, sliced grapes and some salt.

Season the fish fillets with salt and pepper. Put the butter, shallot, fish stock and white wine in a pan (with a tight-fitting lid) over a medium heat. Bring to the boil and boil for 1 minute, then add the seasoned fish fillets and cover with the lid. Check after 3 minutes. The fish should be cooked, but if the fillets are still a little underdone, simply remove the pan from the heat, keeping the lid on, and keep checking after every minute.

While the fish is cooking, gently warm the pickled grape, garlic and parsley dressing to tease out all the flavours.

When the fish is ready, transfer it to warmed plates. Pour the cooking liquor into the dressing and then spoon over the fish. Add the roasted garlic cloves. Serve immediately.

Lemon sole

Lemon sole, to me, is one of the finest flavoured flat fish you can buy. At its best I think it tastes as good, if not better, than a turbot. It also has a melt-in-the-mouth texture, so it's an ideal fish to introduce to young children. Once an under-used fish, it is more popular now that its eating qualities are more widely appreciated; it's also a bit cheaper than most other flat fish. Quite where the name 'lemon sole' comes from is a bit of a mystery. Its flavour is not lemony and it isn't even a sole, belonging instead to the same family as plaice and halibut.

The best time to eat lemon sole is during autumn and winter. The fish should be avoided from April to September when they are spawning, as the roes are very big and the flesh is spongy and not good to eat. We get fantastically fresh lemon sole, landed by day boats and auctioned at Looe's impressive fish market. Cornwall has its own sustainability standards and only allows boats to land that are carrying fish at least 25cm in size. Unfortunately this is not the case elsewhere. Considered a by-catch by many, lemon soles are often caught in an unregulated manner, which increases the chance of undersized fish being landed. They swim in deeper areas and are rarely caught on rod and line. Lemon soles have been known to live to 17 years but most that are sold are around 4 years old. They feed on small crustaceans and barnacles at night, which probably accounts for the shellfish overtones in the delectable flavour of their flesh.

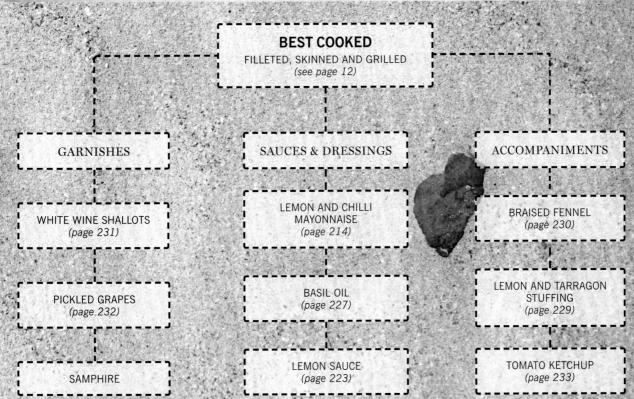

BEST COOKED
FILLETED, SKINNED AND GRILLED
(see page 12)

GARNISHES

SAUCES & DRESSINGS

ACCOMPANIMENTS

WHITE WINE SHALLOTS
(page 231)

LEMON AND CHILLI
MAYONNAISE
(page 214)

BRAISED FENNEL
(page 230)

PICKLED GRAPES
(page 232)

BASIL OIL
(page 227)

LEMON AND TARRAGON
STUFFING
(page 229)

SAMPHIRE

LEMON SAUCE
(page 223)

TOMATO KETCHUP
(page 233)

Lemon sole on the bone with parsley and clam butter

I've always been mad about potted food (shrimps, duck, crab etc), probably because they are so well seasoned, which they need to be as they are typically eaten cold. Here I've taken the classic potted shrimp seasoning – lemon, cayenne, nutmeg and parsley – and incorporated it into butter, which I warm the clams up in. You can do the same with cockles.

Serves 4

4 lemon soles, about 400g each, prepared to cook whole (see page 241)

2kg live clams, cleaned (as for mussels, see page 180)

light rapeseed oil for cooking

100ml white wine

Cornish sea salt

Flavoured butter

250g unsalted butter, softened

4 tsp chopped curly parsley

20 rasps of nutmeg

1 tsp cayenne pepper

finely grated zest and juice of 1 lemon

2 shallots, peeled and finely chopped

1 garlic clove, peeled and finely chopped

To serve

1–2 tbsp chopped parsley

lemon wedges

deep-fried courgettes (page 231), optional

For the flavoured butter, put the butter, parsley, nutmeg, cayenne, lemon zest and juice in a food processor or blender and process for 2 minutes until well blended. Transfer to a bowl and add the shallots, garlic and salt to taste. Fold together until evenly combined. Lay a sheet of cling film on a work surface and spoon the butter onto it. Wrap the butter in the cling film, rolling it into a long sausage and tie the ends of the cling film to secure. Chill for 2 hours to firm up before serving. (The butter will keep in the fridge for a week, or it can be frozen.)

When ready to serve, heat your grill to medium-high. Oil the grill tray. Now oil the white side of the fish, season with salt and lay in the grill tray, white side down. Drizzle a little more oil over the upper brown side of the fish and season with salt. Slide the tray under the grill and cook the fish for 5–6 minutes.

At the same time, place a large saucepan (that has a tight-fitting lid) over a medium heat. When the pan is hot, add the clams and wine. Put the lid on and steam for 2 minutes until the shells open. Drain the clams, reserving the juices; discard any that are unopened.

Baste the fish under the grill with the cooking juices and a little more oil if needed. Grill for a further 5–6 more minutes until cooked, checking every minute or so towards the end.

Meanwhile, unwrap the butter and slice into discs. When the fish is cooked, place 3 slices of the flavoured butter on top of each lemon sole and soften it slightly under the grill. At the same time, gently warm the clams in some of the flavoured butter. (Refrigerate any leftover butter for another use.)

Place a cooked lemon sole on each warmed serving plate and add the fish cooking juices to the clams. Spoon the clams and butter over the lemon soles and sprinkle with some chopped parsley. Serve with lemon wedges and a bowl of crispy deep-fried courgettes or seasonal vegetables of your choice.

Grilled lemon sole with crispy oysters, cucumber, horseradish and lemon

Lemon sole is surprisingly good with oysters, which feature twice in this dish – in the sauce and as deep-fried breadcrumbed nuggets, which provide a crisp contrast in texture. Married with cucumber and horseradish, this has become one of our most popular choices on the menu. On their own, the crispy oysters are a great little snack for a drinks party.

Serves 4 as a starter

1 large lemon sole, about 800g, or 2 smaller 500g fish, filleted and skinned

light rapeseed oil for cooking

Cornish sea salt

Cucumber and horseradish sauce

1 cucumber

50g fresh horseradish, peeled and grated

1 shallot, peeled and diced

50ml white wine vinegar

2 tbsp caster sugar

2 egg yolks

juice of ½ lemon

2 oysters, shucked (see page 258), juices retained

250ml sunflower oil

Cucumber and lemon dressing

2 cucumbers, peeled and diced

2 tsp chopped dill

1 lemon, peel and pith removed, segmented

100ml lemon oil (page 227)

Crispy oysters

4 oysters, shucked (see page 258), juices retained

flour, to dust

1 egg, beaten

100g Japanese panko breadcrumbs

oil for deep-frying

For the cucumber and horseradish sauce, peel the cucumber, cut it in half lengthways, scoop out the seeds, then chop the flesh. Put the horseradish, shallot, wine vinegar, sugar and a pinch of salt into a blender or food processor, add the cucumber and blitz for 3 minutes. Strain through a muslin-lined sieve into a bowl, twisting and squeezing the cloth until you can't extract any more juice. Set aside.

Put the egg yolks, lemon juice and oysters, with their juices (and those from the crispy oysters), into a food processor. Blend for 30 seconds. With the motor running, slowly add the oil until it is all incorporated and you have a thick mayonnaise. Set aside.

For the cucumber and lemon dressing, mix the diced cucumber, chopped dill and lemon pieces together and bind with the lemon oil.

For the crispy oysters, drain the oysters, reserving the juices. Put the flour, beaten egg and breadcrumbs into 3 separate bowls. Pass the oysters through the flour, then the egg and finally the breadcrumbs. Set aside.

Heat your grill to medium-high. Heat the oil for deep-frying in a deep-fryer or other suitable deep, heavy pan to 180°C. Oil the grill tray and sprinkle with salt.

Lay the lemon sole fillets on the tray and place under the grill. They will take no more than 4 minutes to cook; keep a close eye on them to avoid overcooking. At the same time, deep-fry the breaded oysters in the hot oil for 2 minutes until golden.

To finish the sauce, put the cucumber and horseradish stock and the mayonnaise into a pan and whisk together over a low heat; do not allow to boil otherwise the sauce will curdle.

Spoon the sauce equally into 4 warmed bowls and place a breaded oyster on top. Using a palette knife, carefully lay a lemon sole fillet over the oyster and then spoon over the dressing. Serve straight away.

Megrim & witch

Until recently megrim and witch have been pretty much overlooked, but with the demand for something a bit different and cheaper and an increased awareness of sustainability, these members of the sole family have become more popular. Although they are different species they can be quite difficult to tell apart, which is also true of their taste and texture. Commonly found off the Cornish coast, megrim are now often sold as 'Cornish sole'. This sounds quite cool and certainly helps them fly out of the kitchen.

Like all flat fish, megrim and witch live happily at the bottom of the ocean and both are partial to a few little fish. They feed mostly through the summer and are at their best for eating during autumn and winter. Neither of them taste good in the early part of the year when they are spawning. Generally, they are caught a fair way out to sea. I like to cook the 500–600g fish, which should be easy for a good fishmonger to get for you. Both megrim and witch are good for introducing fish to young children as they make lovely posh fish fingers. There are healthy stocks of these soles in our seas, so feel free to cook them often.

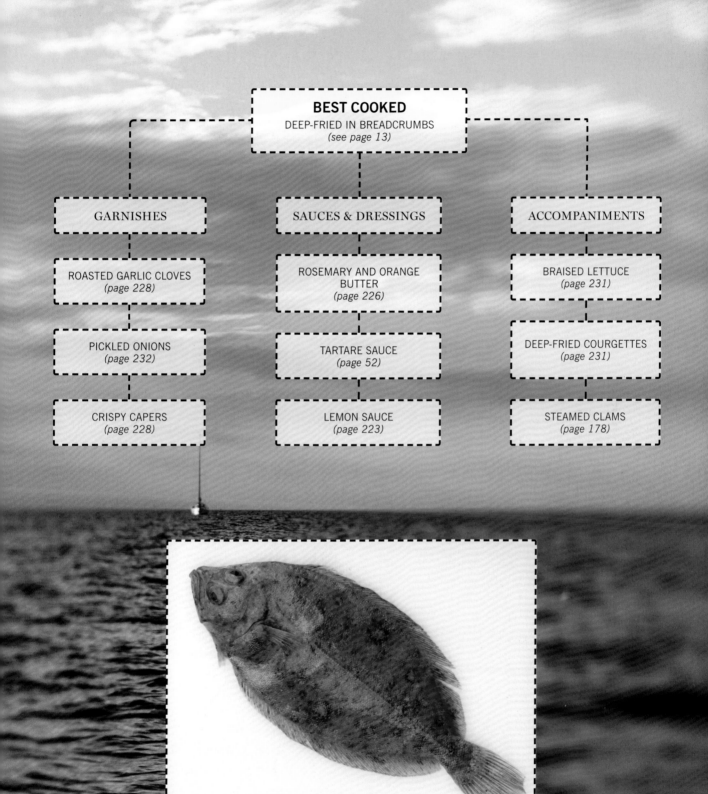

BEST COOKED
DEEP-FRIED IN BREADCRUMBS
(see page 13)

GARNISHES

SAUCES & DRESSINGS

ACCOMPANIMENTS

ROASTED GARLIC CLOVES
(page 228)

ROSEMARY AND ORANGE
BUTTER
(page 226)

BRAISED LETTUCE
(page 231)

PICKLED ONIONS
(page 232)

TARTARE SAUCE
(page 52)

DEEP-FRIED COURGETTES
(page 231)

CRISPY CAPERS
(page 228)

LEMON SAUCE
(page 223)

STEAMED CLAMS
(page 178)

Megrim in a roll with watercress, shallot and tarragon mayonnaise

The idea for this dish came from my fish merchant Tim 'Don' Alsop, who supplies me with great fish from his business at Looe Market. 'Sole in a roll' is on the menu at his seafood eatery, Fish Kitchen. Basically I've nicked his idea, because it tastes so good and it's a brilliant way to serve megrim, although it works with any fish in the ocean.

Serves 4

4 megrim soles, 500–600g each, filleted and skinned

light rapeseed oil for cooking

Cornish sea salt and freshly ground black pepper

Tarragon mayonnaise

1 egg yolk

1 tsp English mustard

4 tbsp chopped tarragon

1 tsp white wine vinegar

250ml olive oil

To serve

poppy and sesame seed rolls (page 234)

olive oil to drizzle

250g watercress, washed and trimmed

red wine shallots (page 231), optional

To make the tarragon mayonnaise, put the egg yolk, mustard, tarragon and wine vinegar into a bowl and whisk for 1 minute to combine. Slowly add the olive oil, drop by drop to begin with, then in a steady stream, whisking constantly, until the mixture is emulsified and thick. Season with a little salt.

To cook the fish, heat your grill to medium-high. Oil the grill tray and sprinkle with salt and pepper. Lay the fillets on the tray and place under the grill. The fish will take no more than 4 minutes to cook; keep a close eye on it to avoid overcooking. The fillets shouldn't need turning as they are thin and the heat from the tray will finish cooking the underside.

Halve your bread rolls and toast under the grill. Drizzle the cut surfaces with some olive oil. Pile some watercress onto the bottom halves and add some red wine shallot rings. Lay the fish fillets on top, add more watercress and shallot rings and finish with a blob of tarragon mayonnaise. Sandwich together with the tops of the rolls. Serve the rest of the mayonnaise in a bowl on the side.

Witch deep-fried in herb and cheese crumbs with tomato and chive salad

Ok, I had to include a dish to appeal especially to children and this is it: deep-fried fish coated in savoury breadcrumbs, served with home-made ketchup and a tomato salad – a guaranteed winner. The cheese makes the coating deliciously crispy and golden. You can use any good mature Cheddar but my favourite is Davidstow as it just happens to be made up the road from my restaurants.

Serves 6

4 witch soles, about 500g each, filleted and skinned

2 eggs, beaten

100g plain flour

oil for deep-frying

Cornish sea salt and freshly ground black pepper

Herb and cheese breadcrumbs

10 slices of white bread, crusts removed

30g flat-leaf parsley

30g chives

30g basil

100g full-flavoured Cheddar, such as Davidstow Crackler, grated

Tomato and chive salad

6 plum tomatoes

12 cherry tomatoes

1 red onion, peeled and finely chopped

2 tbsp chopped chives

75ml extra virgin olive oil

75ml red wine vinegar

pinch of sugar

To serve

tomato ketchup (page 233)

It's best to prepare the tomato and chive salad an hour or so before serving to allow time for the flavours to mingle. Slice the plum tomatoes, halve the cherry tomatoes and place both in a bowl with the red onion, chives, extra virgin olive oil, wine vinegar and sugar. Mix gently and season with salt and pepper to taste.

To make the breadcrumbs, blitz the bread and herbs in a food processor to fine crumbs, then add the cheese and blend for 30 seconds. Spread the crumb mixture out on a tray and cover until ready to crumb the fish.

When ready to serve, arrange the tomato salad on a nice big platter.

Cut the fish fillets in half lengthways. Get ready to crumb the fish: have the beaten eggs in one bowl, the flour seasoned with a touch of salt and pepper in another bowl, and the tray of breadcrumbs to hand. Heat the oil in a deep-fat fryer or other suitable deep, heavy pan to 180°C.

One at a time, dip the fish into the flour, then into the egg and finally in the breadcrumbs to coat. Deep-fry the fish in the hot oil, in batches if necessary, for 3 minutes until golden. Drain on kitchen paper and season with salt.

Place the fish on top of the tomato and chive salad and serve at once, with the tomato ketchup on the side.

Plaice

Distinguished by the orange spots on its green-brown back, plaice has long been one of the most popular flat fish. In season from late April to Christmas, it is a great alternative to its expensive cousins, brill and turbot. Like its cousins, it loves to hide in the sand or shingle and wait for anything edible to come past for its tea. Plaice are particularly fond of mussels and at certain times of the year can be found hanging around areas where mussels are young and relatively easy pickings. Partly for this reason – they much prefer mussels to the fishermen's bait – they are not easy to catch.

Sadly, an awful lot of plaice are caught using heavy beam trawlers, which really takes its toll on the seabed, not to mention the vast by-catch that it sweeps up on the way and the adverse effect on the plaice population. Otter-trawled fish are a better option, if you can get them. Ask your fishmonger where he gets his plaice from.

I much prefer to cook the less fashionable larger plaice, as they have the qualities of brill and can stand up to some big flavours. But be warned… this isn't a fish that needs much cooking and if you do overcook it, it will become very dry and tasteless. Cook with care and you will have beautiful moist white fillets of fish.

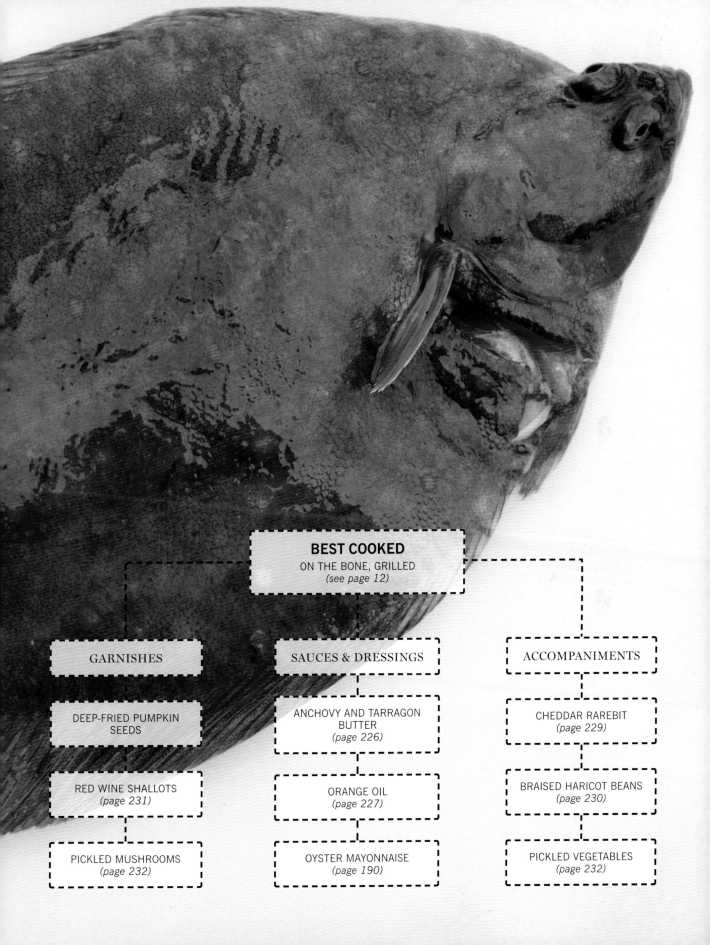

BEST COOKED
ON THE BONE, GRILLED
(see page 12)

GARNISHES

DEEP-FRIED PUMPKIN
SEEDS

RED WINE SHALLOTS
(page 231)

PICKLED MUSHROOMS
(page 232)

SAUCES & DRESSINGS

ANCHOVY AND TARRAGON
BUTTER
(page 226)

ORANGE OIL
(page 227)

OYSTER MAYONNAISE
(page 190)

ACCOMPANIMENTS

CHEDDAR RAREBIT
(page 229)

BRAISED HARICOT BEANS
(page 230)

PICKLED VEGETABLES
(page 232)

Grilled plaice with mustard and tarragon sauce, asparagus and peas

Asparagus and peas are fantastic with fish. Here they are married with mustard and tarragon in a creamy sauce, giving the dish a wonderful array of flavours without compromising the great taste of plaice. A perfect quick, light dinner for a warm spring day.

Serves 4

1 plaice, about 1.5kg, filleted and cut into portions

light rapeseed oil for cooking

1 baby gem lettuce, shredded

16 asparagus spears, blanched and lower part of stems peeled

100g fresh peas, blanched

knob of butter

olive oil to drizzle

Cornish sea salt and freshly ground black pepper

Mustard and tarragon sauce

light rapeseed oil for cooking

2 shallots, peeled and chopped

2 garlic cloves, peeled and chopped

4 tbsp cider vinegar

100ml dry cider

100ml roast fish stock (page 222)

2 tsp wholegrain mustard

100ml double cream

4 tsp chopped tarragon, stalks reserved

2 gherkins, diced

To make the mustard and tarragon sauce, heat a medium saucepan over a medium heat and add a drizzle of oil. Add the shallots and garlic and cook for 1 minute, then add the cider vinegar and reduce right down. Pour in the cider and fish stock and let bubble until the liquid is reduced by half. Now add the mustard, cream and tarragon stalks and simmer to reduce until the sauce is thick enough to coat the back of a spoon. Remove the tarragon stalks. Stir in the diced gherkins and chopped tarragon and set aside.

Preheat your grill to medium. Oil the grill tray and sprinkle with salt. Lay the fish fillets, skin side up, on the tray and place under the grill. Cook for 6 minutes, checking the fish frequently during the last minute or two, to avoid overcooking.

Meanwhile, heat a non-stick pan and add a drizzle of olive oil. When hot, add the lettuce and wilt for 1 minute. Add the asparagus and peas with a knob of butter and warm through for 1 minute. Season with salt and pepper to taste.

When the fish is ready, remove from the grill but leave it on the tray for 2 minutes to allow it to finish cooking in the residual heat. Pour any juices from the tray into the sauce.

To serve, arrange the lettuce, asparagus and peas on 4 warmed plates and carefully place the fish on top. Spoon the sauce around the outside and drizzle a little olive oil over the fish.

Poached plaice, late summer vegetable nage and orange oil

At its best, plaice is wonderful poached and I like to serve it with a medley of fresh vegetables and herbs. Feel free to change the vegetables and herbs as you please, using whatever happens to be in the fridge or garden. You don't necessarily have to use plaice either – any fish will do and you might like to poach a few oysters in there as well.

Serves 4

1 plaice, about 1.5kg, filleted, skinned and cut into 100g portions

100g French beans, trimmed and blanched

100g Swiss chard, trimmed and blanched

4 tomatoes, blanched and skinned

2 tsp chopped tarragon

2 tsp chopped flat-leaf parsley

1 orange, segmented and sliced into small pieces

Cornish sea salt

Vegetable nage

light rapeseed oil for cooking

2 shallots, peeled and finely chopped

4 garlic cloves, peeled and crushed

1 fennel bulb, trimmed, halved and sliced

150ml white wine

200ml vegetable stock (page 222)

200ml roast fish stock (page 222)

100ml double cream

To finish

drizzle of orange oil (page 227)

For the vegetable nage, place a fairly wide saucepan over a medium heat and add a drizzle of oil. When hot, add the shallots, garlic and fennel and cook, stirring, for 2 minutes – just to soften the vegetables a little. Add the wine and let it bubble to reduce almost completely. Now add both stocks and simmer until reduced by half. Add the cream and bring to a simmer. Taste and season with salt if required. Set aside.

Season the plaice fillets with salt, roll them and gently lower into the nage. Bring back to a simmer and simmer gently for 1 minute, then remove from the heat. Leave to stand for 3 minutes; the fish will finish cooking in the residual heat.

When the fish is ready, using a fish slice, carefully transfer the fillets to a warmed plate; keep warm. Add the beans, chard, tomatoes and herbs to the nage. Set aside 4 orange segments for the garnish and add the rest to the nage. Bring back to a simmer.

Divide the vegetables and nage equally between 4 warmed bowls. Top with the plaice fillets and finish with the reserved orange segments and a drizzle of orange oil. Serve at once.

Turbot

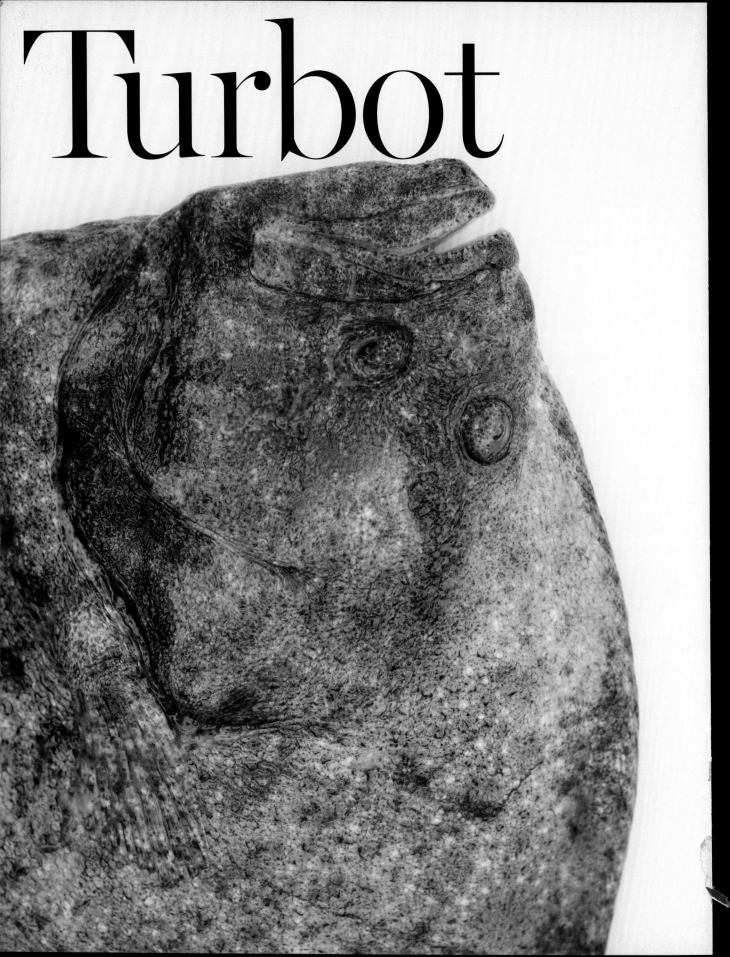

Turbot is the king of the sea. Great tasting, very expensive and becoming rather hard to get hold of, it has long been revered. It is welcome on any menu, albeit often with a staggering price tag. The largest of the flat fish, turbot is related to brill, flounder and plaice.

Turbot starts life as a round fish, feeding off plankton. After the first 6 months it gradually transforms itself into a flat fish, becoming a 'bottom feeder' that loves to eat small fish and crustaceans. Like other flat fish, turbot are adept at camouflage, blending in with their environment. This enables them to hunt lazily, by staying still on the seabed and waiting for dinner to arrive.

Turbot are very rarely caught off the shore with rod and line, so most are landed from boats. Unfortunately some of our turbot is captured with heavy trawling gear that runs along the bottom of the seabed, breaking up the natural ecosystem for other species of seafood to grow and live in. Seek out line-caught turbot, which is perfectly acceptable to eat. Farmed turbot is another option and not a bad one in my view; in fact it is pretty good. Turbot is at its peak when the water and weather is cold. I'd recommend avoiding it during the spawning season from late spring through the summer when the roes are very big. Apart from the reduced quality, you'll be paying for that extra weight of roes.

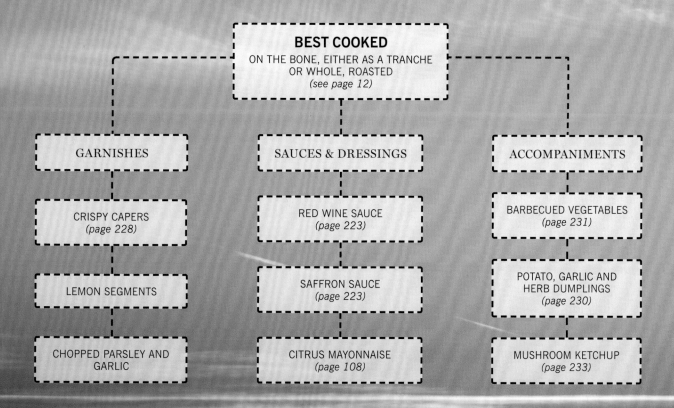

BEST COOKED
ON THE BONE, EITHER AS A TRANCHE
OR WHOLE, ROASTED
(see page 12)

GARNISHES

SAUCES & DRESSINGS

ACCOMPANIMENTS

CRISPY CAPERS
(page 228)

RED WINE SAUCE
(page 223)

BARBECUED VEGETABLES
(page 231)

LEMON SEGMENTS

SAFFRON SAUCE
(page 223)

POTATO, GARLIC AND
HERB DUMPLINGS
(page 230)

CHOPPED PARSLEY AND
GARLIC

CITRUS MAYONNAISE
(page 108)

MUSHROOM KETCHUP
(page 233)

Turbot in a bag with parsley and cockle butter dressing

This is probably the best way to cook turbot. A hot oven and plenty of butter brings out the best of its natural flavour and gives you the base for a fantastic dressing. You can use mussels, clams or any other shellfish in place of cockles, and vary the herbs if you like – try chervil, fennel or dill in place of parsley.

Serves 6

1 turbot, at least 2kg, cut into 6 tranches (see page 242)

1kg live cockles, cleaned (see page 173)

olive oil for cooking

2 shallots, peeled and chopped

2 garlic cloves, peeled and chopped

200g salted butter, in pieces

2 handfuls of chopped flat-leaf parsley

100ml white wine

juice of 1 lemon

Cornish sea salt and freshly ground black pepper

To serve (optional)

braised lettuce (page 231)

Heat your oven to 220°C/gas 7. Take a baking tray large enough to hold the turbot tranches comfortably. Lay 6 large pieces of non-stick baking parchment side by side on a work surface and lightly oil them in the middle. Place a turbot tranche in the centre of each piece of oiled parchment and sprinkle evenly with the shallots, garlic, butter and most of the chopped parsley. Season the fish with salt and pepper.

Draw up the edges of the paper and fold them together, leaving a little opening in the middle. Pour the white wine and lemon juice through each opening and then seal the parcels. Cook in the oven for 10 minutes, then take out the tray and carefully cut open the paper at the top.

Scatter the cockles over the fish and scrunch up the paper to re-seal. Place back in the oven for 2–3 minutes until the cockles open up; discard any unopened ones.

Carefully lift the turbot and cockles in the paper onto warmed plates. The cooking juices from the bags provide the dressing – just add a bit more chopped parsley if you wish. Serve with lemon wedges. Braised lettuce is a lovely accompaniment to this dish.

Turbot with tartare sauce 'my way'

I prepared this dish for BBC2's Great British menu, because I wanted to show that the familiar taste of fish and chips can take centre stage at any special occasion. The judges thought it was great and I really have to agree! The sauce is my interpretation of the classic tartare.

Serves 4

1 turbot, about 1.5kg, filleted, skinned and cut into 150g portions, trimmings saved for goujons

50g plain flour

1 egg, beaten

150g Japanese panko breadcrumbs

100g potatoes, such as Maris Piper, peeled and diced

oil for deep-frying

light rapeseed oil for cooking

Cornish sea salt and freshly ground black pepper

Tartare sauce

1 egg yolk

1 tsp English mustard

1 tsp white wine vinegar

250ml olive oil

50ml double cream

100ml hot roast fish stock (page 222)

2 gherkins, diced

1 tsp each chopped chervil, chives, parsley and tarragon

To finish

1 baby gem lettuce, shredded

100g peas, blanched

50g crispy capers (page 228)

50ml lemon oil (page 227)

For the goujons, cut the turbot trimmings into 2cm wide strips. Have the flour, egg and breadcrumbs in 3 separate bowls and season the flour with salt. Pass the goujons through the flour, then the egg and finally roll in the breadcrumbs to coat all over. Set aside until ready to cook.

Simmer the diced potatoes in salted water for about 7 minutes until barely tender. Drain, refresh in cold water and set aside.

To make the sauce, put the egg yolk, mustard and wine vinegar into a bowl and whisk for 1 minute to combine. Slowly add the olive oil, drop by drop to begin with, then in a steady stream, whisking constantly, until the mixture is emulsified and thick. Season this mayonnaise with a little salt.

When ready to serve the fish, finish the sauce. Add the cream to the mayonnaise, then slowly whisk in the hot fish stock, until the sauce is thick enough to just coat the back of a spoon. Add the lettuce and peas to the sauce and heat through for 1 minute. Finally add the diced gherkins and chopped herbs. Season with salt and pepper to taste. Put to one side.

Heat the oil for deep-frying in a deep-fryer or other suitable deep, heavy pan to 180°C. Deep-fry the potato cubes for 4 minutes until crispy and golden. Drain on kitchen paper and keep warm. Lower the oil temperature to 160°C.

Heat a frying pan and add a drizzle of oil. When hot, add the turbot portions and season with a little salt. Cook gently for 4–5 minutes until the fish is lightly golden at the edges. Carefully flip the fish over and remove the pan from the heat. The gentle residual heat will finish the cooking process.

In the meantime, deep-fry the goujons in the hot oil for 2–3 minutes until golden, then remove with a slotted spoon, drain on kitchen paper and season with a little salt.

Spoon the tartare sauce into 4 warmed bowls, piling the peas and lettuce in the centre. Place the turbot fillets on top and arrange the potatoes around the edge. Garnish with the goujons and crispy capers, and add a drizzle of lemon oil if you wish. Serve at once.

Round
white
fish

Bream

Sea bream has a lovely flavour and texture, yet it is so often overlooked. When guests order this fish, whether it's black or gilthead bream, they are generally surprised at how good it is. Black bream is caught all around the UK's south and southwest coastline and recently wild giltheads have been landed too. Black bream is plentiful, sustainable and at its best during the summer, so don't miss out. Black bream are great fun to catch from small inshore boats using light tackle. They have strong, powerful teeth, which they use to rip mussels off rocks, so that's where you'll find them lurking. They are also attracted to the bait in lobster and crab pots, and have a healthy appetite for seaweed. Just make sure you return any immature fish less than 23cm long. And avoid black bream altogether during the spring spawning season.

If you come across gilthead bream on a menu, it is much more likely to be farmed. To me, it is no less special. The flesh is similarly firm and flavourful, cooks well and is very tasty. If you are lucky enough to get wild black bream do buy them, otherwise farmed gilthead is an excellent option. All of my recipes work with both species. If you are preparing a whole fish, beware of the sharp spines along the fins and around the gills – cut them off with scissors before you begin. If you are pan-frying, grilling or barbecuing bream, aim for a crispy skin – it is truly delicious.

BEST COOKED
FILLETED AND PAN-FRIED
(see page 12)

GARNISHES	SAUCES & DRESSINGS	ACCOMPANIMENTS
PINK GRAPEFRUIT SEGMENTS	SAFFRON SAUCE *(page 223)*	BARBECUED VEGETABLES *(page 231)*
RED PEPPER MARMALADE *(page 152)*	PARSLEY, LEMON AND GARLIC DRESSING *(page 224)*	SPICED PICKLED VEGETABLES *(page 232)*
PICKLED ONIONS *(page 232)*	CURRIED CRAB MAYONNAISE *(page 200)*	BRAISED FENNEL *(page 230)*

Roasted bream with rosemary and orange butter

Whole bream is a great fish for the barbecue but if the weather's not up to it, then a hot oven will do the trick instead. Bream handles big bold flavours well and because the flesh has a slightly oily edge, rosemary is a good companion. I love the pairing of orange and rosemary, especially with this type of fish, but feel free to use any herb or other citrus here.

Serves 4

4 bream, about 400g each, fins and gills cut off, scaled and gutted

olive oil for cooking

8 rosemary sprigs, washed

Cornish sea salt and freshly ground black pepper

Flavoured butter

2 tbsp chopped rosemary

1 shallot, peeled and chopped

2 garlic cloves, peeled and chopped

finely grated zest of 1 orange

250g unsalted butter, softened

To serve

rosemary sprigs to garnish

pickled vegetables (page 232), optional

To make the flavoured butter, put the chopped rosemary, shallot, garlic and orange zest into a bowl. Add the softened butter and mix together with a spatula until evenly blended. Season with salt and pepper to taste. Lay a sheet of cling film on a work surface and spoon the butter onto it. Wrap the butter in the cling film, rolling it into a long sausage, and tie the ends of the cling film to secure. Chill for 2 hours before using.

If you are barbecuing the fish, light your barbecue well ahead. Otherwise heat your oven to 220°C/Gas 7 and put a lightly oiled roasting tray inside to heat up. Lay the bream on a board and score both sides with a sharp knife at 2cm intervals. Stuff 2 rosemary sprigs into the cavity of each fish. Oil the fish all over and season with salt and pepper.

Lay the fish on the barbecue or roasting tray and cook for 8 minutes, then turn and cook on the other side for a further 6–8 minutes. Remove from the heat, turn the fish over again and rest for a few minutes. Meanwhile, cut 16 slices from the flavoured butter.

Lay 4 slices of butter on each fish and give it another minute on the barbecue or in the oven. Transfer to a warmed platter and spoon over any juices from the roasting tray. Garnish with fresh rosemary. I like to serve this with my pickled vegetables and a rocket or watercress salad on the side.

Pan-fried bream with spring vegetable nage

Vegetable nage was on the opening menu at my first restaurant Black Pig in Rock. I would throw in any veg I could get my hands on and the herbs were freshly picked from our herb patch. Topped with a fillet of wild black bream it became a signature dish. You can vary it with the seasons, making it simple or complex. I like it to have a medley of vegetables, so every spoonful promises a different taste, texture and look.

Serves 4

2 bream, about 500g each, fins and gills cut off, scaled, gutted, filleted and pin-boned

Spring vegetable nage

finely pared zest and juice of 1 lemon

400ml vegetable stock (page 222)

12 asparagus spears, trimmed

100g podded peas

light rapeseed oil for cooking

2 shallots, peeled and chopped

1 garlic clove, peeled and chopped

4 young carrots, peeled and sliced

1 fennel bulb, trimmed and chopped

100ml double cream

4 small spring onions, trimmed and sliced

1 tsp chopped mint

1 tsp chopped chervil

1 tsp chopped tarragon

Cornish sea salt and freshly ground black pepper

To finish

lemon oil (page 227)

For the nage, place a saucepan over a medium-low heat to heat up, then add the lemon zest. Heat for a minute to allow the lemon zest to release its natural oils and then pour in the vegetable stock. Bring to the boil, lower the heat and simmer for 5 minutes. Set aside to cool. Once cooled, add the lemon juice.

To cook the vegetables for the nage, blanch the asparagus and peas in boiling salted water for a few minutes until just tender, then drain and refresh in cold water; drain and set aside. Heat a little rapeseed oil in a saucepan and add the shallots and garlic. Sweat for 1 minute, without colouring, then add the carrots and fennel. Continue to sweat for another 2 minutes and then add the nage stock. Simmer until the carrots start to soften slightly, about 5 minutes. Now add the cream and simmer for a couple of minutes. Season with salt and pepper to taste.

To cook the fish, heat a large non-stick frying pan and add a drizzle of oil. Once the oil is hot, place the fish in the pan, skin side down, and cook for 2 minutes or until the skin is golden and crisp at the edges. Flip the fish over and take the pan off the heat. The fish will continue to cook in the residual heat while you finish the nage.

To finish the nage, add the blanched asparagus and peas, spring onions and herbs and simmer for 1 minute. Ladle the vegetables and nage into 4 warmed soup plates. Top with the pan-fried fish, placing it skin side up, and drizzle the lemon oil around. Serve at once.

Poached bream with piccalilli spices, broccoli and spinach

This dish was conceived over an after-service beer with the restaurant team. Piccalilli is one of our favourite condiments and we often pair it with ham and other meats, but never fish. We decided to lighten the spices and try it with bream. The result was magnificent... finished with smoked oil it is one of our favourite dishes.

Serves 4

2 bream, 500–600g each, fins and gills cut off, scaled, gutted, filleted, skinned and pin-boned

16 tenderstem broccoli stems

100ml roast fish stock (page 222)

200g baby spinach, washed

2 tbsp white wine shallots (page 231)

Cornish sea salt and freshly ground black pepper

Cure and spice paste

1 tsp cayenne pepper

1 tsp ground ginger

1 tbsp ground turmeric

1 tbsp mustard seeds

100g sea salt

2 garlic cloves, peeled and chopped

1 tbsp English mustard

200ml white wine vinegar

200ml water

100g caster sugar

Poaching sauce

1 egg yolk

1 tsp English mustard

1 tsp white wine vinegar

250ml olive oil

50ml double cream

To finish

smoked oil (page 227)

For the cure and spice paste, in a bowl, mix together the cayenne, ginger, turmeric and mustard seeds. Put half of the mixture into a medium saucepan. Add the sea salt to the rest and mix well.

Sprinkle the spiced salt evenly over the 4 fish fillets and place in the fridge for 1 hour to cure.

Meanwhile, add the garlic, mustard, wine vinegar, water and sugar to the spice mix in the pan and bring to the boil over a medium heat. Let bubble to reduce down to a thin paste consistency, stirring every so often to make sure it doesn't catch. Pour into a small bowl and reserve.

Once the fish has been curing for an hour, wash off the spiced salt and pat dry. Refrigerate until needed. Blanch the broccoli in boiling salted water for 2 minutes, then drain and refresh in cold water; drain and set aside.

To make the poaching sauce, whisk the egg yolk, mustard and wine vinegar together in a bowl, then slowly whisk in the olive oil to emulsify (as for a mayonnaise). Finally, whisk in the cream and 2 tsp of the reserved spice paste; set aside.

Cut the bream fillets into 2cm dice. Bring the fish stock to the boil in a pan. Once boiling, add the reserved spice paste followed by the fish and remove the pan from the heat. Leave to stand for 2 minutes to allow the fish to cook in the residual heat. Now remove the fish with a slotted spoon to a warmed dish; keep warm.

Whisk enough of the hot fish stock into the poaching sauce to give a pouring consistency. Return to the pan and place over a low heat to warm through; do not allow to boil. Add the spinach to the sauce and heat for 1 minute to barely wilt, then add the fish, white wine shallots and blanched broccoli. Warm for a further minute. Taste and adjust the seasoning with salt and pepper as necessary.

Ladle the fish, vegetables and sauce into warmed bowls, drizzle each portion with a little smoked oil and serve immediately.

The nation's favourite fish has undoubtedly suffered for its popularity. Overfishing for decades has decimated the cod population and although stocks have improved a bit in recent years with greater awareness of the problem, we still need to use discretion when buying this fish, otherwise it could disappear altogether. Cod come inshore to breed between February and April and these breeding stocks have been particularly vulnerable. We really must avoid the fish at these times. Cod are usually caught when they are 3–5 years old, but they can reach 50 years or more if they manage to avoid predators, especially humans. In the water, cod are not particularly impressive. Rather than hunt, they just hang around waiting for their lunch to come along. In fact, they're pretty lazy really. When you're fishing, you can usually tell when you've caught a cod, because it puts up the briefest of fights, then gives up, so reeling one in is a piece of cake.

Cod

Cod has delicately flavoured, flaky white flesh. Because almost all of its oil is stored in its liver, the flesh has virtually no fat and is very high in protein, which is obviously great for you. However, in my experience it is a fish that needs to be eaten very fresh, as it seems to lose its light, delicate nature relatively quickly. I tend to salt my cod in sea salt for 30 minutes just to firm up the flesh and get rid of the excess water. A light salting also seems to bring out much more of the natural flavour.

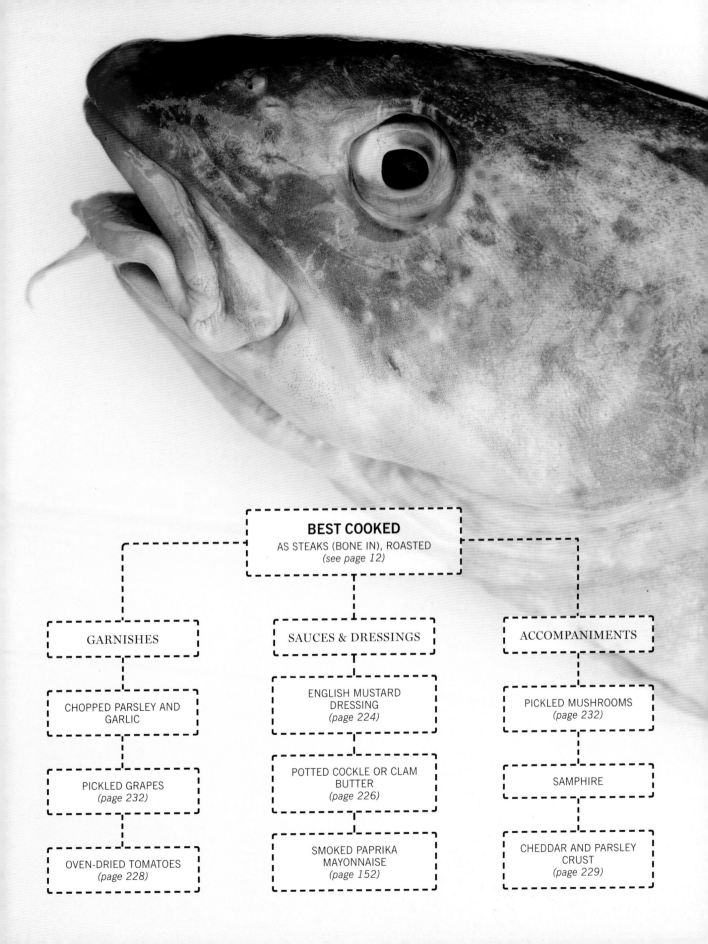

BEST COOKED
AS STEAKS (BONE IN), ROASTED
(see page 12)

GARNISHES

SAUCES & DRESSINGS

ACCOMPANIMENTS

CHOPPED PARSLEY AND
GARLIC

ENGLISH MUSTARD
DRESSING
(page 224)

PICKLED MUSHROOMS
(page 232)

PICKLED GRAPES
(page 232)

POTTED COCKLE OR CLAM
BUTTER
(page 226)

SAMPHIRE

OVEN-DRIED TOMATOES
(page 228)

SMOKED PAPRIKA
MAYONNAISE
(page 152)

CHEDDAR AND PARSLEY
CRUST
(page 229)

Baked cod steak with portabella mushrooms, red onions and thyme

This is a great informal dish. The small amount of prep involved can be done in advance and you can take the dish straight from the oven to the table. Cutting cod into steaks and roasting it on the bone is a good way to get the most from your fish as all the flavour is retained and there is virtually no wastage.

Serves 2–3

1 cod, about 1kg, scaled, gutted and cut into 3 steaks (see page 249)

olive oil for cooking

2 red onions, peeled and cut into wedges, root end intact

3 garlic cloves (unpeeled)

3 portabella or large field mushrooms, cut into 2cm thick slices

6 thyme sprigs

100ml white wine

Cornish sea salt and freshly ground black pepper

To serve

mushroom ketchup (page 233)

Heat your oven to 200°C/Gas 6. Lightly oil an ovenproof dish that will comfortably hold the fish steaks. Lay the onions, garlic and mushrooms in the dish and scatter over the thyme sprigs. Drizzle with olive oil and season with salt and pepper. Cook in the oven for 10 minutes.

Take the dish from the oven. Season the cod steaks all over with salt and pepper, then place on top of the vegetables and pour over the wine. Place in the oven for 12–14 minutes until the fish is just cooked.

Serve straight from the dish with the mushroom ketchup and a big bowl of seasonal salad leaves on the side. As you tuck into the fish, don't forget to spoon out all those lovely cooking juices in the bottom of the dish and squeeze out the sweet garlic from the skins. Share the third cod steak if serving two.

Roast cod on celeriac and apple soup with apple and thyme dressing

I love a really good vegetable soup with a nice big chunk of fresh fish in the middle – it's a brilliant meal in one. Here the cod is lightly salted first, to give the whole dish a bit more texture and flavour. The earthy taste of celeriac marries perfectly with the zingy fresh apple and aromatic thyme, creating a wonderful soup to showcase the fish.

Serves 4

600g cod fillet

100g sea salt

light rapeseed oil for cooking

Cornish sea salt and freshly ground black pepper

Soup

light rapeseed oil for cooking

100g butter

1 large celeriac, peeled and roughly chopped into 2cm dice

about 300ml vegetable or roast fish stock (page 222)

3 tart English eating apples, peeled, cored and finely sliced

juice of ½ lemon

Apple and thyme dressing

1 tsp chopped thyme

1 tsp white wine shallots (page 231)

30ml cider vinegar

100ml light olive oil

1 crisp dessert apple

Lay the fish in a dish and sprinkle evenly with the sea salt. Cover with cling film and refrigerate for 30 minutes. Wash off the salt, pat the fish dry on kitchen paper and cut into 4 portions. Wrap each portion tightly in cling film and refrigerate for at least 2 hours to firm up.

To make the soup, heat up a big saucepan over a medium heat, then add a drizzle of oil and the butter. Once the butter is sizzling, add the celeriac and cook for 2 minutes without colouring. Now add 100ml of the stock, cover and cook for 5 minutes. Check if the celeriac is cooked; if not add a little more stock if it seems dry and simmer until tender – you are aiming for cooked celeriac and minimum liquid. Once the celeriac is cooked, add the sliced apples to the pan and cook for a further 3 minutes until they have broken down.

Tip the contents of the pan into a blender and process until smooth. Season with salt to taste and reserve the purée until ready to serve.

To make the apple and thyme dressing, combine the chopped thyme, white wine shallots and cider vinegar in a bowl and whisk in the olive oil. Season with salt to taste and set aside to allow the flavours to marry together. Shortly before serving, peel, core and dice the apple and add to the dressing.

When ready to cook the fish, heat your oven to 200°C/Gas 6.

Place an ovenproof non-stick frying pan over a medium heat. When the pan is hot, add a little oil and place the fish in the pan, skin side down. Cook for 2 minutes until the skin starts to golden. Turn the fish over and transfer to the oven to finish cooking for 4 minutes.

While the fish is in the oven, heat up the celeriac purée in a saucepan over a medium heat, adding more of the stock until you have the required soup consistency, whisking to combine. Season with salt to taste.

To serve, pour the soup into 4 warmed soup plates. Place a portion of cod, skin side up, in the centre of the soup and finish with a spoonful of dressing over and around the fish.

Cod 'BLT'

This is a great dish to enjoy as a robust salad on a warm summer's evening in the garden. The cod works so well with the light fresh taste of the tomato and the crisp grilled bacon introduces a nice salty element. I like to serve the dish just warm, flaking the cod over the salad at the last minute.

Serves 4

1 cod, about 1.5kg, scaled, gutted, filleted and skinned

4 rashers of smoked streaky bacon

light rapeseed oil for cooking

8 cherry tomatoes, halved

Cornish sea salt and freshly ground black pepper

BLT sauce

8 vine-ripened tomatoes

2 garlic cloves, peeled and chopped

30ml white wine vinegar

1 tbsp sugar

1 red chilli, deseeded and chopped

3 egg yolks

1 tsp English mustard

1 tsp white wine vinegar

300ml light olive oil

50ml double cream

To serve

2 baby gem lettuces, washed and roughly torn

8 oven-dried tomatoes (page 228)

2 tsp white wine shallots (page 231)

10 basil leaves, roughly torn

Well in advance, make the tomato stock for the sauce. Chop the tomatoes and put them into a bowl with the garlic, wine vinegar, sugar and chilli. Season with a little salt and mix well. Lay a large piece of muslin over a bowl, leaving plenty overhanging the sides. Tip the tomato mixture into the muslin cloth. Now bring the four corners of the muslin together over the bowl and tie securely. Suspend the muslin bag over the bowl in the fridge and allow the tomato stock to drip through into the bowl overnight or for at least 6 hours.

In the meantime, lay the fish fillets in a dish and sprinkle evenly with about 50g sea salt. Wrap in cling film and refrigerate for 30 minutes to lightly salt the fish. Wash off the salt and pat the fish dry on kitchen paper. Wrap tightly in cling film and refrigerate for at least 2 hours to firm up.

To make the BLT sauce, whisk the egg yolks, mustard and wine vinegar together in a bowl, then slowly whisk in the olive oil to emulsify (as for a mayonnaise). Finally, whisk in the cream.

When ready to cook the fish, heat your grill to medium-high. Cook the bacon on the grill rack until crispy on both sides. Remove and cut into small pieces. Set aside; keep warm.

Oil the grill tray and season it with salt. Place the fish on the tray with the cherry tomatoes. Drizzle with a little oil and sprinkle with a little salt. Slide the tray under the grill and cook for 6 minutes until the fish is almost cooked, just a little underdone.

In the meantime, arrange the lettuce over a large platter and scatter over the oven-dried tomatoes and white wine shallots. Whisk the tomato stock into the sauce and heat gently in a saucepan on a low heat, whisking all the time; do not allow to boil.

Flake the cod over the lettuce, add the cherry tomatoes and sprinkle on the crispy bacon and torn basil. Spoon the sauce over the cod and salad and serve straight away.

There are three types of this amazing and strange-looking fish: the red, the grey and the tub. The red is the most common and the smallest, the grey is the biggest and the tub is the rarest. All are very sustainable and most certainly fish that we should be eating more of. They are at their best for eating from late summer until the end of the winter; avoid them during the spring and early summer spawning season. The gurnard has an interesting feeding pattern, as it eats whatever it fancies from wherever. It uses its almost hand-like fins to feel around on the seabed looking for little prawns, crabs and lobsters, but also likes to have a go at chasing small fish.

Gurnard

Gurnard, also known as sea robins or crooners, make a funny crocking noise when you land them on your boat, which most often happens by accident. The ones I've caught have always been on fishing trips for mackerel – it's a joy and surprise to all on the boat when you pull one in. They also happen to be very tasty cooked along with the mackerel on the barbecue the same day.

Gurnard is a real treat to eat, but perhaps owing to its scary appearance, it's taken a while to become properly appreciated in the kitchen. Its creamy-white, firm flesh has an excellent texture and subtle flavour. So, if you get a chance to buy gurnard, go for it.

BEST COOKED
AS FILLETS, GRILLED SKIN SIDE UP
(see page 12)

GARNISHES

ORANGE SEGMENTS

OVEN-DRIED TOMATOES
(page 228)

WHITE WINE SHALLOTS
(page 231)

SAUCES & DRESSINGS

SAFFRON SAUCE
(page 223)

ROSEMARY AND ORANGE
BUTTER
(page 226)

SQUID INK MAYONNAISE
(page 216)

ACCOMPANIMENTS

TOMATO KETCHUP
(page 233)

BRAISED FENNEL
(page 230)

PICKLED CHICORY
(page 22)

Red gurnard soup with samphire and orange

Fish soups are a great way to start a special meal. This is my take on a soup I tasted years ago, which was made with a whole red mullet. The flavour was amazing, though personally I thought it was a waste to pulp the fish flesh for the broth. Here I pan-fry the gurnard fillets and serve them on top of the soup with fragrant, salty samphire and a punch of zingy orange. It tastes as good as it looks...

Serves 4

2 gurnard, about 700–800g each, scaled, gutted, filleted and pin-boned (heads and bones reserved)

light rapeseed oil for cooking

2 white onions, peeled and chopped

2 carrots, peeled and chopped

1 red chilli, deseeded and chopped

1 red pepper, cored, deseeded and chopped

4 garlic cloves, peeled and crushed

1 tbsp good quality tomato purée

10 ripe tomatoes, chopped

1 bay leaf

1 rosemary sprig

finely pared zest and juice of 1 orange

1 litre roast fish stock (page 222)

200g samphire, washed and trimmed

1 small orange, peel and pith removed, segmented

Cornish sea salt and freshly ground black pepper

Heat a medium-large saucepan over a medium heat. When hot, add a drizzle of oil, then the onions, carrots, chilli, red pepper and garlic. Cook for 5 minutes to soften, stirring every minute to avoid the vegetables catching. Next add the fish bones and heads, along with the tomato purée, and cook for another 5 minutes, stirring again every minute.

Now add the tomatoes, bay leaf, rosemary sprig and orange zest and juice. Cook for a further 5 minutes, giving the mixture a good stir every couple of minutes. Pour in the fish stock and bring to a simmer. Lower the heat and cook for 20 minutes.

Pass the soup through a mouli or a large potato ricer into another saucepan. (If you don't have a mouli or potato ricer, you can blitz the soup in a blender, then pass it through a sieve but you won't achieve quite the same clarity.) Taste the soup and correct the seasoning with salt and pepper. Keep warm over a low heat.

To cook the samphire, add to a pan of boiling water, bring back to the boil and cook for 1 minute; drain and keep warm.

To cook the fish, heat a non-stick frying pan over a medium heat. When hot, add a little oil and place the fillets in the pan, skin side down. Cook for 3 minutes until the skin starts to crisp up, then flip the fish over and cook for a further 1 minute. Take off the heat, keeping the fish in the pan to finish cooking in the residual heat as you serve up the soup.

Divide the soup between warmed soup plates, scatter half of the samphire in the centre and place the fish on top. Finish with the remaining samphire and a few pieces of orange. Serve at once.

Red gurnard with mushrooms, garlic, parsley and oven-dried tomatoes

Gurnard is a fish that can handle big bold flavours. It has a fairly subtle taste, which is greatly enhanced by ingredients that marry well. Here the combination of pickled mushrooms, parsley and garlic works with the sweet, slightly acidic semi-dried tomatoes to bring out the best in the gurnard.

Serves 4

4 gurnard, about 600g each, scaled, gutted, filleted and pin-boned

1 red onion, peeled and chopped

4 garlic cloves, peeled and chopped

100ml red wine vinegar

50g caster sugar

100ml red wine

150g unsalted butter

1 thyme sprig

50ml olive oil

400g Japanese cultivated mushrooms, like shiitake, shimeji or oyster

1 shallot, peeled and chopped

light rapeseed oil for cooking

1 quantity oven-dried tomatoes (page 228)

2 tsp chopped flat-leaf parsley

Cornish sea salt and freshly ground black pepper

To serve

1 bunch of watercress, washed and trimmed

2 tsp red or white wine shallots (page 231)

Put the red onion, a quarter of the garlic, half of the red wine vinegar, the sugar and red wine into a small saucepan. Bring to the boil over a medium heat and let bubble until the liquor is well reduced and syrupy, then remove from the heat and let cool.

Meanwhile, put the butter into another pan with another quarter of the garlic and the thyme. Melt over a medium heat and simmer until the butter starts to bubble and turn a light brown colour. Remove from the heat and allow to cool and settle.

To cook the mushrooms, heat a large non-stick frying pan. When hot, add the olive oil followed by the mushrooms. Cook for 2 minutes, stirring all the time. Tip in the shallot and half the remaining chopped garlic and cook for a further minute. Add the rest of the red wine vinegar, stirring to deglaze the pan, and season with salt and pepper to taste. Remove the mushrooms to a tray and set aside.

To cook the fish, heat a non-stick frying pan over a medium heat. When hot, add a little oil and place the fillets in the pan, skin side down. Cook for 3 minutes until the skin starts to crisp up, then flip the fish over and cook for a further 1 minute. Take off the heat, but keep the fish in the pan to finish off the cooking.

In a medium pan, add 4 tbsp of the red wine reduction to the brown butter, followed by the mushrooms, remaining garlic, oven-dried tomatoes and chopped parsley. Warm through gently over a low heat and taste for seasoning, adding salt and pepper as needed.

Divide the watercress between 4 plates and scatter over the pickled shallot. Arrange the fish fillets on top and spoon on the mushrooms, tomatoes and dressing. Serve at once.

Haddock

Haddock, like cod, is one of those unfortunate fish in such high demand that it's been overfished for decades. Commercial trawling is largely to blame for the depleted population. Haddock grows much more slowly than its fish and chip mate cod, which exacerbates the problem, and it doesn't grow as big as its cousin either. However, increasingly, haddock are line caught, which is a much more sustainable method. Line-caught fish are usually tagged by fisherman, but if it's not clear how the haddock you are buying has been caught, look for scales – if there are plenty still on the fish, the chances are it's been line caught.

To find their dinner of crustaceans and small fish, haddock feel around the ocean bed with their barbule, which hangs from the lower jaw and looks like a 'goaty beard'. Haddock can live for up to 20 years and are best eaten in the summer and autumn. In the winter they move off to deeper waters to spawn in the colder temperatures. Most of the haddock eaten in the UK is landed in northern ports, but I've caught them in Cornwall a few times on my mackerel feathers, along with cod and whiting. I'd say they are not the hardest of fish to catch, unless you are looking to target a big one. When buying haddock from your fishmonger, I'd recommend you only do so if it is line caught, otherwise substitute pollack, pouting or coley.

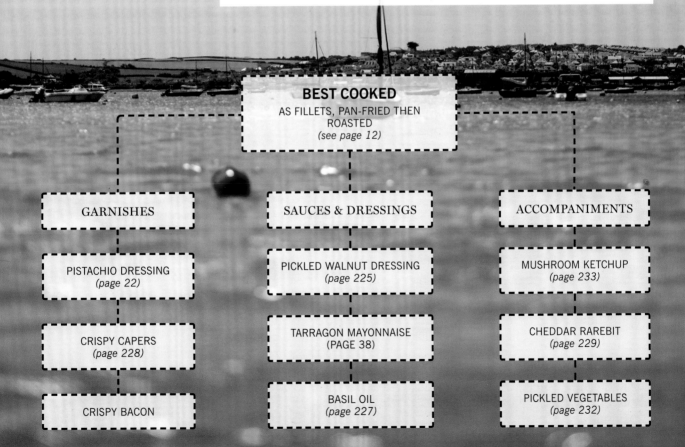

BEST COOKED
AS FILLETS, PAN-FRIED THEN ROASTED
(see page 12)

GARNISHES	SAUCES & DRESSINGS	ACCOMPANIMENTS
PISTACHIO DRESSING *(page 22)*	PICKLED WALNUT DRESSING *(page 225)*	MUSHROOM KETCHUP *(page 233)*
CRISPY CAPERS *(page 228)*	TARRAGON MAYONNAISE *(PAGE 38)*	CHEDDAR RAREBIT *(page 229)*
CRISPY BACON	BASIL OIL *(page 227)*	PICKLED VEGETABLES *(page 232)*

Rosemary cured haddock with tomatoes, watercress and ketchup

This dish came about, as many of my dishes do, from bringing together three great ingredients in season at the same time. My fish merchant Tim brought in some stunning young haddock when the garden was full of ripe tomatoes and fragrant with rosemary. All I needed to do was marry them together. Include the potato dumplings for a more substantial dish; leave them out if you just want a nice simple fish salad.

Serves 4

4 haddock fillets, about 200g each, skinned and pin-boned

8 tsp sea salt, plus extra to season

4 tsp chopped rosemary

20 cherry tomatoes, halved

1 shallot, peeled and chopped

1 garlic clove, peeled and chopped

50ml olive oil

20g caster sugar

2 tsp red wine vinegar

light rapeseed oil for cooking

To serve

potato, garlic and herb dumplings (page 230), optional

small bunch of watercress, washed and trimmed

tomato ketchup (page 233)

Place the fish on a tray. Mix the 8 tsp salt and rosemary together and sprinkle evenly all over the fish, turning to coat both sides. Cover and place in the fridge for 1 hour.

Wash the rosemary salt off the fish and pat dry. If salting in advance, wrap very tightly in cling film and refrigerate – this will give the fish a lovely shape when you cook it. Otherwise set the fillets aside until ready to cook.

Put the cherry tomatoes into a shallow dish and add the shallot, garlic, olive oil, sugar, wine vinegar and a pinch of salt. Toss to mix and leave to marinate for at least 1 hour at room temperature.

To cook the fish, heat your oven to 200°C/Gas 6. Heat an ovenproof non-stick frying pan over a medium heat, then add a drizzle of oil. When hot, add the fish to the pan and cook for 2 minutes. Once the fish starts to turn golden underneath, transfer the pan to the oven and cook for 4 minutes.

If serving the dumplings, while the fish is in the oven pan-fry them in a little oil to finish (see page 230). When the fish is ready, remove the pan from the oven and flip the fillets over. They will finish cooking in the residual heat.

Divide the watercress and marinated tomatoes between 4 plates, adding the dumplings, if serving, and spoonfuls of tomato ketchup. Lay the haddock fillets on top and serve at once, with the remaining ketchup on the side.

Grilled haddock with a salad of cauliflower, apples and chestnuts

This is one of the Seafood and Grill's most popular dishes. It is perfect during the autumn, when fresh chestnuts or cobnuts are around. The combination of raw cauliflower, seasonal apple, crunchy chestnuts and chives in a mustardy dressing is great with haddock grilled on the bone. Try it with crunchy pear instead of apple, too... equally delicious.

Serves 4

4 haddock steaks, about 250g each

Cornish sea salt and freshly ground black pepper

Cauliflower purée and salad

1 medium-small cauliflower

light rapeseed oil for cooking

50g unsalted butter

2 crunchy green eating apples

200g fresh chestnuts, roasted and peeled (or roasted shelled cobnuts)

2 tbsp chopped chives

about 100ml English mustard dressing (page 224)

First prepare the cauliflower. Cut off the base and divide the cauliflower into florets. Slice these lengthways thinly, with a sharp knife. Put a quarter of the cauliflower into a bowl and set aside for the salad; use the rest for the purée.

To make the cauliflower purée, heat a saucepan over a medium heat and add a drizzle of oil and the butter. When the butter has melted, add the cauliflower and cook, stirring, for 2 minutes, without colouring. Add just enough water to cover the cauliflower, bring to a simmer and put the lid on. Cook for 10 minutes or until tender, checking the water level occasionally and adding a little more if needed. Drain the cauliflower, then purée in a food processor or blender until smooth. Transfer to a bowl or pan, cover and keep warm.

To prepare the cauliflower, apple and chestnut salad, halve, core and thinly slice the apples. Roughly chop the roasted nuts. Add both to the sliced cauliflower with the chives.

Heat your grill to medium and lightly oil the grill tray. Season the haddock with salt and pepper and place on the grill tray. Slide the fish under the grill and cook for 5 minutes. Check to see if the fish is cooked – it should come away from the bone. If not, continue grilling, checking every minute. Remember that fish continues to cook after it is taken from the heat, so is best removed a little undercooked.

Spoon the warm cauliflower purée onto 4 warmed plates. Dress the cauliflower salad with the mustard dressing and place next to the purée. Place a haddock steak on each portion of cauliflower purée and drizzle over any cooking juices from the tray. Serve at once.

Hake

This has got to be one of the most fearsome and ugly looking fish in the sea, but you can never judge a book by its cover… Hake is a delicious fish and in prime condition has a unique eating quality. Chunky and soft, it has a very moist mouth-feel and is great simply roasted or grilled and enjoyed on its own.

Hake is from the same family as cod, but is very different in physique and temperament. With a mouth full of sharp, pointed teeth and a long, slender body, it really is a hunting machine. The best time to eat hake is from September to December; avoid it during the spring and early summer spawning season.

On spring tides in Cornwall hake is landed locally at Newlyn, where our merchants bid for it, generally losing out to the Spanish who go crazy for this fish. In fact the Spanish obsession with hake has seriously depleted stocks. It is one of those fish that doesn't live once it is caught so you won't see it in an aquarium. There is no point throwing hake back once it's landed so we should at least do it justice by eating it. If you have never tried it, I'd recommend buying a 2kg hake to cook whole and serve as a centrepiece at the table, but do make sure it has been sustainably caught.

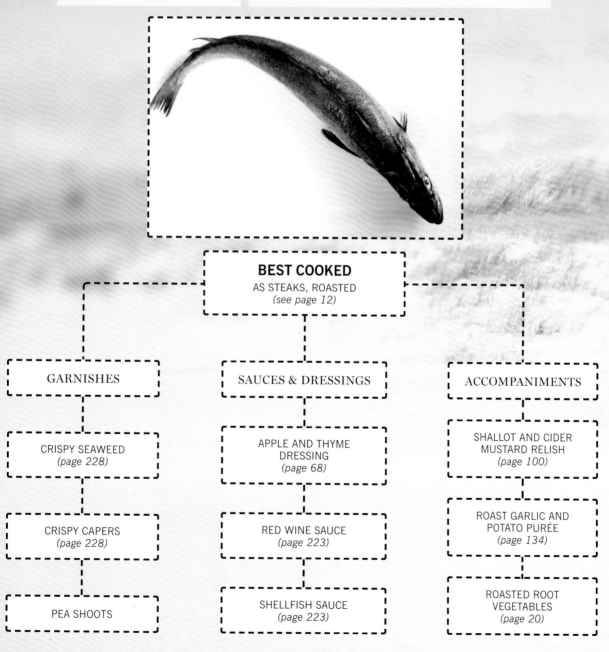

BEST COOKED
AS STEAKS, ROASTED
(see page 12)

GARNISHES

CRISPY SEAWEED
(page 228)

CRISPY CAPERS
(page 228)

PEA SHOOTS

SAUCES & DRESSINGS

APPLE AND THYME
DRESSING
(page 68)

RED WINE SAUCE
(page 223)

SHELLFISH SAUCE
(page 223)

ACCOMPANIMENTS

SHALLOT AND CIDER
MUSTARD RELISH
(page 100)

ROAST GARLIC AND
POTATO PURÉE
(page 134)

ROASTED ROOT
VEGETABLES
(page 20)

Hake fish fingers with Pete's chips, mushy peas and herb emulsion

Fish fingers and chips... This is where my love of seafood started – not with oysters or a platter of *fruits de mer* in France, but with the ubiquitous yellow box of Captain Bird's Eye fish fingers. Here is my version – probably the best fish fingers and chips you'll ever taste! The mushy peas and herb emulsion are lovely, but my head chef Pete's chips are truly amazing. You can use other white fish, such as pouting or pollack.

Serves 6

1kg hake fillet, skinned and pin-boned

1kg potatoes, ideally Maris Piper, peeled

100g plain flour

2 eggs, beaten

100g Japanese panko breadcrumbs

oil for deep-frying

Cornish sea salt and freshly ground black pepper

Herb emulsion

2 medium egg yolks

25g full-flavoured Cheddar, such as Davidstow, finely grated

1 tsp English mustard

1½ tsp cider vinegar

1 tbsp chopped chives

1 tbsp chopped tarragon

250ml sunflower oil

Mushy peas

1kg frozen peas

2 tsp chopped mint

2 tsp chopped tarragon

50g butter

50ml white wine vinegar

To serve

2 lemons, cut into wedges

First make the herb emulsion. Put the egg yolks into a blender or food processor with the cheese, mustard, cider vinegar, chopped chives and tarragon. Process for 1 minute and then slowly pour in the oil while the motor is still running. Once it is all incorporated, stop the blender and season with a little salt to taste. Transfer to a bowl, cover and refrigerate.

For the chips, cut the potatoes into wedge-shaped chips, about 2cm wide and 5cm long. Boil in simmering salted water until tender and almost starting to break up. Drain and leave to cool on a tray until required.

For the mushy peas, add the frozen peas to a pan half-filled with boiling water, bring back to the boil and simmer for 2 minutes. Drain well and tip into a blender or food processor. Add the chopped herbs, butter and wine vinegar and process briefly, retaining some texture. Transfer the mushy peas to a bowl or small pan and keep warm.

Cut the fish fillet into strips, about 1cm wide and 4cm long. Pass the fish fingers through the flour, then the egg and finally through the breadcrumbs to coat evenly all over. Heat the oil in a deep-fat fryer to 180°C.

To finish the chips, immerse in the hot oil and fry until golden, then drain on kitchen paper and season with salt. Fry the fish in the hot oil for 3 minutes until golden, then similarly drain and season with salt.

Pile the fish fingers and chips onto a large warmed serving platter. Place in the centre of the table, with the mushy peas, pot of herb emulsion and lemon wedges, so everyone can help themselves.

Salt hake with squid ink, parsley and tomato and garlic sauce

Salting fish in this way draws out some of the water and improves the flavour and texture, giving you a much meatier mouth-feel. It works particularly well with hake. Try blending a little spice or the grated zest of any citrus fruit with the salt to bring your own touch to this dish.

Serves 4

4 hake portions, about 200g each, filleted and pin-boned

2 medium squid, prepared (see page 262) and cut into rings

100g sea salt

2 garlic cloves, peeled

2 tsp chopped parsley

olive oil for cooking

100g peeled, deseeded butternut squash, cut into 1cm dice

1 leek, trimmed (white part only), washed and cut into 1cm pieces

1 Dutch red chilli, deseeded and chopped

4 spring onions, trimmed and sliced

Cornish sea salt and freshly ground black pepper

Tomato and garlic sauce

500ml roast fish stock (page 222)

4 ripe tomatoes, skinned, deseeded and chopped

4 garlic cloves, peeled and crushed

3 tsp squid ink, or more to taste

50g unsalted butter

To finish

extra virgin olive oil

Lay the fish on a tray large enough to hold the portions side by side, without overlapping. Sprinkle evenly with the sea salt, turning to coat both sides, then cover with cling film and refrigerate for 30 minutes. Wash the salt off the fish, then pat dry on kitchen paper and wrap each portion tightly in cling film. Refrigerate for at least 2 hours to firm up, preferably overnight.

To make the tomato and garlic sauce, put all the ingredients into a saucepan and bring to a simmer. Let bubble until the liquid has reduced to a quarter of its original volume. Transfer to a blender or food processor. Blitz for 4 minutes to emulsify the sauce and thicken it slightly. Set aside until ready to serve.

Heat your oven to 200°C/Gas 6. Chop the 2 garlic cloves, then add the chopped parsley and chop together; reserve until serving.

Heat a large non-stick pan over a medium heat and add a drizzle of olive oil. When hot, add the squash and cook, stirring, for 3 minutes. Add the leek, chilli and spring onions and cook for a further 3 minutes, stirring and adding a little more oil if it looks dry. Season with salt and pepper. Once the squash is cooked, transfer the vegetables to a warmed dish; keep warm.

Heat a large ovenproof non-stick frying pan over a medium heat and add a drizzle of oil. When hot, place the fish in the pan, skin side down, and cook for 2 minutes. Transfer to the oven and cook for a further 3 minutes.

While the fish is cooking, place another frying pan over a medium heat and add a little olive oil. When hot, add the squid and cook for 1 minute; don't move it about much – let it take on some colour. Add 1 tsp of the chopped garlic and parsley and take off the heat. Season with salt and pepper.

Reheat the sauce gently on the hob; if it isn't dark enough for you, whisk in a little more squid ink. Take the fish out of the oven as soon as it is ready. Flip it over and allow it to finish cooking in the residual heat of the pan.

Divide the vegetables between 4 warmed plates and top with the squid. Place the hake alongside and sprinkle with the remaining parsley and garlic. Spoon the sauce around and finish with a drizzle of extra virgin olive oil.

John

Now some say ugly, I say unusual. John Dory is one of my favourite fish to cook. It's a treat, because it isn't always available and sometimes you don't see it for ages. In the UK, as far as I'm aware, there aren't any fishermen that target John Dory; it is more of a by-catch, and what a gem it is. This fish is an amazing hunter. Because of its almost invisible head-on appearance, it swims up, opens its huge mouth and swallows its prey whole, in a flash. It also has some pretty good defence mechanisms. The large dark mark on its side looks to other fish like a giant eye – some say it was bestowed by Saint Peter as he was pulling the fish from the sea of Galilee at Christ's request, hence its nickname Saint Peter's fish. It also has some very sharp, almost barbed, thorns on its body and sharp fins.

Dory

John Dory is unique in that it yields six fillets, three on each side, which are not the easiest to fillet off the bone, but worth the effort. It can also be pretty expensive, but don't let that put you off. John Dory can be found around most of Britain's coastline, but the majority is caught in the Southwest – off wrecks and with trawl nets. The best time to eat it is from September until early spring; avoid it in late spring and summer when the fish are breeding. Also resist smaller fish, under 35cm, as these haven't yet reached the stage where they have been able to breed. Basically, if you get a chance to eat or buy John Dory, do so, because its texture and appearance are so different from any other fish. In my view, it's fantastic.

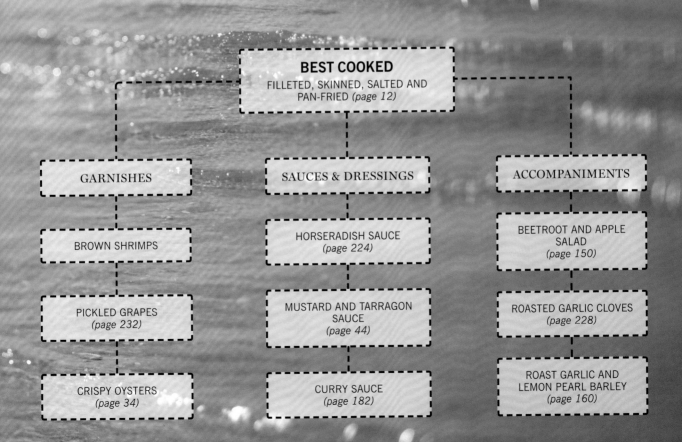

BEST COOKED
FILLETED, SKINNED, SALTED AND
PAN-FRIED *(page 12)*

GARNISHES	SAUCES & DRESSINGS	ACCOMPANIMENTS
BROWN SHRIMPS	HORSERADISH SAUCE *(page 224)*	BEETROOT AND APPLE SALAD *(page 150)*
PICKLED GRAPES *(page 232)*	MUSTARD AND TARRAGON SAUCE *(page 44)*	ROASTED GARLIC CLOVES *(page 228)*
CRISPY OYSTERS *(page 34)*	CURRY SAUCE *(page 182)*	ROAST GARLIC AND LEMON PEARL BARLEY *(page 160)*

Marinated John Dory with sea buckthorn and wild fennel

John Dory, like many other fish, is lovely eaten raw if it's very fresh. Instead of the typical citrusy dressing I'm using sea buckthorn, a wild berry that grows by the water's edge close to our restaurant. Its sharp taste – a cross between orange and passion fruit – is perfect for the marinade. Wild fennel, which grows locally too, lends a special quality. You can buy sea buckthorn juice online or from healthfood shops.

Serves 4

2 John Dory, about 1kg each, filleted and skinned

50ml sea buckthorn juice

2 tbsp honey

1 small shallot, peeled and finely chopped

1 garlic clove, peeled and finely chopped (central green germ discarded)

1 tsp English mustard

100ml sunflower oil

2 fennel bulbs, trimmed

3 tsp chopped wild fennel or fennel herb

mustard cress to garnish

olive oil to drizzle

Cornish sea salt and freshly ground black pepper

Using a very sharp knife, cut the fish into very fine slices and arrange them on a platter, overlapping them as little as possible.

For the marinade, whisk the sea buckthorn juice, honey, shallot, garlic and mustard together in a bowl. Slowly, drop by drop, whisk in the sunflower oil until it is all incorporated, then season with a pinch of salt.

Spoon most of the dressing evenly over the fish, making sure you cover each piece; reserve a little of the dressing for the shaved fennel. Cover the fish and leave to marinate in the fridge for 1 hour.

In the meantime, finely slice the fennel bulbs into wafer-thin slivers, using a mandolin if you have one. Toss with the remaining dressing.

Sprinkle the wild fennel or herb over the marinated fish and then scatter the fennel slivers over the top. Finish with the mustard cress and a drizzle of olive oil.

John Dory with mussels in cumin and apple sauce

Very fresh John Dory retains its lovely, moist texture and amazing pearly white flesh if you grill it, providing you keep a close eye – overcook it and the texture will be ruined. Mussels and cumin pair well and apple lends a touch of sweetness, creating a unique fresh-tasting sauce that works brilliantly with this fish.

Serves 4

2 John Dory, about 1kg each, or 4 smaller 600g fish, filleted and skinned

1kg live mussels, cleaned (see page 180)

100ml dry white wine

olive oil to drizzle

12 tenderstem broccoli stems

Cornish sea salt and freshly ground black pepper

Cumin and apple sauce

1 tbsp olive oil

2 small onions, peeled and finely chopped

2 leeks, trimmed (white part only), washed and thinly sliced

2 garlic cloves, peeled and crushed

2 apples, peeled, cored and diced

2 tsp ground cumin

500ml shellfish stock (page 222)

500ml roast fish stock (page 222)

4 ripe tomatoes, skinned, deseeded and chopped

50g unsalted butter

First make the sauce. Heat a large saucepan and add the olive oil. When hot, add the onions, leeks, garlic and apples. Sweat for 2 minutes, then add the cumin and cook gently for a further 5 minutes or until the vegetables are starting to colour, but don't allow them to darken. Pour in both stocks, add the tomatoes and butter and bring to a steady simmer. Let bubble until the liquid has reduced down to a quarter of its original volume. Transfer to a blender or food processor and blitz for 4 minutes, to emulsify the sauce and thicken it slightly. Set aside until ready to serve. (The sauce can be cooled and kept in the fridge for up to 3 days, if preparing ahead.)

To cook the mussels, place a large saucepan (one with a tight-fitting lid) over a medium heat. When hot, add the mussels and wine and immediately clamp the lid on. Cook for 2 minutes to steam the mussels open. Remove the lid and check if the mussels are open; if not cook them for a further ½–1 minute. Drain the mussels in a colander over a bowl to catch the liquor; discard any that have not opened. Pick the mussels from their shells and add them to the sauce.

To cook the fish, heat the grill to medium and lightly oil the grill tray. Trim the John Dory fillets as necessary and lay them on the grill tray. Drizzle with olive oil and season with salt. Place the fish under the grill for 6 minutes until just cooked.

Meanwhile, blanch the broccoli in boiling salted water for 3 minutes or until just tender. Gently reheat the mussel sauce, bringing it to a low simmer.

Divide the sauce between warmed plates. Carefully lift the fish from the grill tray and place on the sauce. Drain the broccoli and arrange around the fish. Serve at once.

Ling

Ling is one of the biggest fish I've ever prepared and an awkward one at that. It is the largest member of the cod family, but in structure it has the head of a cod and the body of a conger eel, so it looks like a cross between the two fish. I think the taste is great and the texture is firm and meaty – more akin to monkfish than any of the cod family. The best time to eat this relatively inexpensive fish is during the winter when the water is colder. They spawn during the spring and early summer, so don't eat them then. Ling feed lazily off the seabed and they will eat almost anything. I've come across all sorts preparing them, even a coin!

Ling are very slow growing fish and don't usually breed until they are 5 years old. So sustainability is a concern, particularly as ling have been heavily fished in deep water using beam trawlers. Inshore line-caught fish are a much better option. Check with your fishmonger how his ling has been caught. A good size fish to buy is about 1–1.5kg. Avoid fish less than 80cm as these won't have had a chance to breed.

BEST COOKED
FILLETED, SKINNED, SALTED AND PAN-FRIED
(see page 12)

GARNISHES

SAUCES & DRESSINGS

ACCOMPANIMENTS

CHOPPED PARSLEY AND GARLIC

ORANGE OIL
(page 227)

BIG CHIPS

CRISPY SEAWEED
(page 228)

BARBECUE SAUCE
(page 106)

PICKLED MUSHROOMS
(page 232)

CRISPY MUSSELS
(page 182)

TARRAGON, LEMON AND MUSTARD BROWN BUTTER
(page 114)

SAMPHIRE

Ling with squid, fennel and salami salad and orange oil

The great thing about this recipe is that it gives you two dishes in one: a roasted piece of succulent ling on wilted chard and a salad of squid, salami, fennel and orange; or you can serve the fish simply with the fennel and orange salad, leaving out the squid and salami. An anise flavoured salami is particularly good here, but any will do. You can use lemon oil in place of the orange if you prefer.

Serves 4

4 ling fillets, about 200g each, pin-boned

200g squid, prepared into rings, tentacles and wings (see page 262)

olive oil for cooking

200g Swiss chard, stems removed, and washed

Cornish sea salt and freshly ground black pepper

Fennel and salami salad

2 fennel bulbs, trimmed (tough outer layer removed)

1 orange, peel and pith removed, segmented

20 slices of salami

2 tsp chopped chives

about 5 tbsp orange oil (page 227)

For the salad, finely slice the fennel, using a mandolin if you have one. Immerse in iced water for 20 minutes, to firm up and crisp the fennel. Drain the fennel, pat dry and place in a bowl with the orange segments.

When ready to cook and serve, heat your oven to 200°C/Gas 6. Heat a large ovenproof frying pan that can take all the fish fillets and add a drizzle of olive oil. When hot, add the fish, skin side down, and cook for 2 minutes until the skin starts to turn golden. Lay the salami slices over the fish and place in the oven for 3 minutes.

Meanwhile, heat another frying pan over a high heat. When the frying pan is hot, add a drizzle of olive oil followed by the squid. Fry for 1 minute, then season with salt and pepper. Tip the squid into the bowl with the fennel and orange segments.

When the fish is ready, remove from the oven and add the salami to the fennel and squid salad with the chives. Toss the salad together, season with salt and pepper and dress with orange oil to taste.

Heat a frying pan and add a little oil. When hot, add the Swiss chard and wilt for 2 minutes, seasoning with salt to taste.

Divide the wilted chard between 4 warmed plates, placing it on one side. Arrange the salad on the other side and lay the fish on top of the chard. Finish with a little drizzle of orange oil.

Ling burger with shallot and cider mustard relish

I enjoy doing food festivals. Recently I was asked to run a stall selling fast-cooked food in our style, so I came up with these spicy ling burgers. We made 300 and sold out within 3 hours! They really are that good, so do try them. Great for the barbecue...

Makes 10 burgers

1.5kg ling fillet, skinned, pin-boned and diced

olive oil for cooking

6 banana shallots, peeled and roughly chopped

8 garlic cloves, peeled and finely chopped

3 medium-hot red chillies, deseeded and finely diced

5 tbsp chopped flat-leaf parsley

3 eggs, lightly beaten

250g fresh white breadcrumbs

Cornish sea salt and freshly ground black pepper

Shallot and cider mustard relish

olive oil for cooking

4 banana shallots, peeled and finely chopped

200ml cider vinegar

1 litre dry cider

3 tsp chopped thyme

200g caster sugar

4 apples, peeled and chopped

5 tbsp wholegrain mustard

To serve

cider bread rolls (page 235)

200g rocket leaves, washed

3 beef tomatoes, sliced

100g red wine shallots (page 231)

First make the relish. Heat a little olive oil in a large pan and sweat the shallots for 2 minutes over a medium heat. Add the cider vinegar, cider, thyme and sugar. Heat, stirring until the sugar is dissolved, then bring to the boil. Let bubble to reduce until the liquor becomes syrupy. Add the chopped apples and cook until they are soft. Stir in the mustard and season with salt and pepper to taste. Transfer to a jar with a tight-fitting lid and leave to cool before sealing. (This relish will keep in the fridge for a couple of months.)

To make the burgers, heat a frying pan over a medium heat and add a drizzle of olive oil. Sweat the shallots, garlic and chillies for 2 minutes, then remove to a plate and allow to cool.

Working in 2 batches, blitz the ling in a food processor for 1 minute, then transfer to a large bowl. Add the shallot and chilli mixture, the parsley, eggs, breadcrumbs and some salt and pepper. Mix well, using your hands, until evenly mixed and well combined. At this stage it is best to fry off a little piece to taste for seasoning, then you can adjust the mixture, adding salt and pepper as necessary. When you are happy with the taste, divide the mixture into 100g balls and mould them into patties. Lay on a tray and refrigerate until ready to cook.

To cook the burgers, heat your oven to 200°C/Gas 6. Heat a frying pan over a medium heat and add a good drizzle of olive oil. When hot, add the patties and fry for 2 minutes on each side. Transfer them to a baking tray and place in the oven for 3 minutes to finish cooking.

Meanwhile, split your rolls in half. Drizzle the bottom halves with a little olive oil, then add some rocket leaves and a slice or two of tomato. Take the patties from the oven and place on the tomato. Add a few red wine shallots and a generous spoonful of shallot and cider mustard relish. Sandwich together with the tops of the rolls and serve with extra dressed rocket leaves and tomatoes on the side.

Salt ling with razor clams, bacon and onion and bay purée

A few years ago I prepared this dish for a nerve-wracking demonstration to 300 chefs in London. I wanted to show that something as unsophisticated as ling is good enough for any menu, not merely a cheap fish to bulk out fish cakes. It worked a treat. The razor clams and seaweed bring the dish to life with their different aromas and textures, and the onion and bay purée give it a rich finish.

Serves 4

4 ling fillets, about 200g each, skinned and pin-boned

8 razor clams, well rinsed

4 tbsp sea salt

50ml white wine

olive oil for cooking

Cornish sea salt and freshly ground black pepper

Sauce

2 shallots, peeled and finely diced

2 garlic cloves, peeled and chopped

6 celery sticks, peeled and cut into 1cm dice

1 carrot, peeled and cut into 1cm dice

100ml roast fish stock (page 222)

50ml double cream

Onion and bay purée

50g unsalted butter

2 large white onions, peeled and chopped

3 bay leaves

400ml Sharp's Doom Bar beer (or other bitter)

To serve

200g sea beet or spinach

4 rashers of smoked streaky bacon, grilled and chopped

2 tsp chopped parsley

crispy seaweed (page 228)

Lay the fish fillets on a tray and sprinkle evenly all over with the sea salt. Cover with cling film and refrigerate for 1 hour. Wash off the salt under cold running water and pat the fish dry on kitchen paper. Wrap each fillet tightly in cling film and chill for at least 2 hours to firm up.

For the onion and bay purée, heat a medium pan, then add a drizzle of oil and the butter. Sweat the onions over a medium heat, stirring, until coloured. Add the bay leaves and cook for a further 2 minutes, then pour in the beer and reduce right down, almost to nothing. Tip into a blender and blitz until smooth. Season with salt and pepper to taste. Set aside.

To cook the razor clams, heat a wide, shallow saucepan (that has a tight-fitting lid) over a medium heat. When hot, add the razor clams and white wine and clamp the lid on. Cook for 2–3 minutes to steam the clams open. Remove from the pan and let cool a bit. Clean the clams (see page 259) and cut into 1cm pieces, reserving the juices and shells. Refrigerate until needed.

Next make the sauce. In a saucepan, sweat the shallots, garlic, celery and carrot in a little olive oil over a medium heat for 5 minutes. Add the fish stock and cook until the carrots start to soften slightly. Add the cream and reserved clam juice and simmer for 5 minutes. Season to taste. Keep warm.

To cook the fish, heat a non-stick frying pan over a medium heat, then add a drizzle of oil. When hot, place the fish in the pan. Cook for 3 minutes, then flip the fillets over and cook for 2 minutes on the other side. Take off the heat; the fish will finish cooking in the residual heat.

While the fish is cooking, heat a little olive oil in a saucepan, add the sea beet and cook for 2 minutes until just wilted. Season with salt and pepper.

To serve, gently reheat the onion and bay purée. Spoon 2 tbsp into the centre of each warmed plate. Reheat the sauce and add 2 tbsp of the purée, the clams, bacon and chopped parsley. Lay the reserved clam shells on the plates and spoon in the clam mixture. Spoon the sea beet alongside and place the fish on the purée and sea beet. Finish with the crispy seaweed.

Monkfish

Also known as anglerfish, this is an ugly beast to say the least. With its huge head in comparison to its body, strange evil-looking face and wide mouth full of razor-sharp teeth, it's enough to scare any angler. Extending from the top of its head are flexible spines with nodules on the ends, which look like tasty small fish swimming about in the water. These glow in the dark and attract prey, even in murky storm conditions. The unfortunate fish swim up readily, undeterred by the monkfish's gigantic head as it resembles a giant rock and blends in perfectly with the environment. All the monkfish needs to do is lie in wait for dinner… hunting doesn't get much easier.

Perhaps because of its unfortunate appearance, it took a while for humans to warm to this fish. Fifty years ago it would most likely have ended up in a tin of cat food, but over the years chefs and home cooks have come to appreciate its attributes. Monkfish has a great taste, lovely meaty texture and is extremely versatile, not least because it can handle lots of different flavours. And with only one central bone to contend with, this is a pretty easy fish to prepare.

Sadly, increasing popularity has led to monkfish's decline, not least because it has been subject to beam trawling. Another issue is that it dies when brought on board and cannot be returned. Monkfish are quite slow growing and live for a long time. You really should avoid them in late spring as this is when they spawn. My favourite way to cook monkfish is on the bone – on a charcoal barbecue or under the grill. Monkfish livers are amazing to eat, so if you get a chance, do buy them and use to make a tasty pâté or pan-fry and eat on toast.

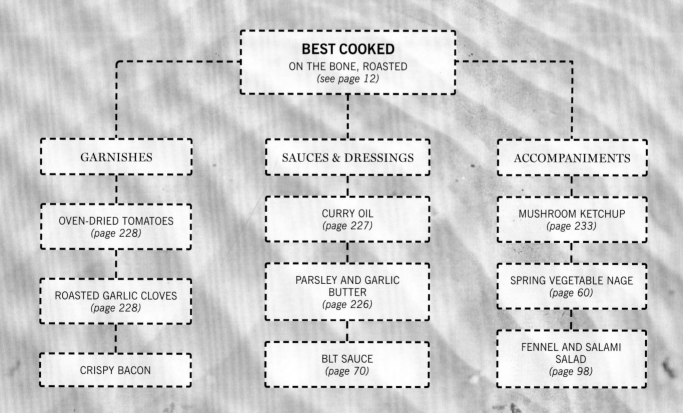

BEST COOKED
ON THE BONE, ROASTED
(see page 12)

GARNISHES

OVEN-DRIED TOMATOES
(page 228)

ROASTED GARLIC CLOVES
(page 228)

CRISPY BACON

SAUCES & DRESSINGS

CURRY OIL
(page 227)

PARSLEY AND GARLIC
BUTTER
(page 226)

BLT SAUCE
(page 70)

ACCOMPANIMENTS

MUSHROOM KETCHUP
(page 233)

SPRING VEGETABLE NAGE
(page 60)

FENNEL AND SALAMI
SALAD
(page 98)

Monkfish on the bone, barbecue style

Firm-textured monkfish stands up well to the heat of the barbecue, but you can grill it instead if you like. The predominant flavours in the barbecue sauce – orange and rosemary – work so well here, though I tweak the flavourings according to what I have to hand and which fish I happen to be cooking. I like to serve this with a medley of barbecued vegetables, which I cook just before the monkfish.

Serves 4

4 monkfish tails on the bone, about 300g each, trimmed of sinew and skin

olive oil for cooking

Barbecue sauce

olive oil for cooking

2 shallots, peeled and chopped

8 garlic cloves, peeled and chopped

3 green chillies, deseeded and chopped

1 bunch of tarragon, leaves picked and chopped

8 rosemary sprigs, leaves picked and chopped

1 small bunch of parsley, leaves picked and chopped

3 tbsp fennel seeds

grated zest and juice of 2 oranges

150g caster sugar

150ml red wine vinegar

250ml orange juice (from a carton is fine)

3 tsp English mustard

150g tomato ketchup (page 233)

Cornish sea salt and freshly ground black pepper

To serve (optional)

barbecued vegetables (page 231)

To make the barbecue sauce, heat a frying pan over a medium heat and add a drizzle of olive oil. When hot, add the shallots, garlic and chillies and sweat for 2 minutes. Add the herbs, fennel seeds and orange zest and cook for another minute. Next add the sugar and wine vinegar, stir until the sugar is dissolved, then let bubble to reduce until syrupy. Now add the orange juice (including the freshly squeezed), mustard and tomato ketchup. Bring to a simmer and let bubble until the liquid has reduced by half. Taste and season with salt and pepper as required. Tip the contents of the pan into a food processor and blitz for 2 minutes. Strain through a sieve into a bowl and leave to cool. This sauce will keep in the fridge for a week.

A couple of hours before cooking the fish, lay the monkfish tails side by side in a dish and spoon 2 tbsp of the barbecue sauce over each one. Cover and leave to marinate for 2 hours.

Light your barbecue well ahead, or preheat the grill to medium-high just before cooking. When hot, cook the fish for 5 minutes on each side or until it just starts to come away from the bone; do not overcook.

Serve the fish on warmed plates with some fresh sauce and barbecued vegetables, if you like, on the side.

Monkfish 'scampi', citrus mayonnaise and root vegetable salad

Back in the days when 'scampi in a basket' was all the rage, breaded monkfish was sometimes passed off as scampi. It seemed a good solution, if illegal, as the price of Dublin Bay prawns escalated in the quest to provide breaded scampi for the masses. This is my mock take: light morsels of crumb-coated monkfish served with a crunchy root vegetable salad and a citrus mayonnaise to give a zing of freshness.

Serves 6

1 kg trimmed monkfish fillet

100g plain flour

2 eggs, beaten

200g Japanese panko breadcrumbs

Cornish sea salt and freshly ground black pepper

Citrus mayonnaise

3 egg yolks

1 tsp English mustard

1 garlic clove, peeled and finely chopped

1 tsp white wine vinegar

finely pared zest of 1 lemon, finely chopped

finely pared zest of 1 orange, finely chopped

300ml light olive oil

Root vegetable salad

2 carrots, peeled

1 celeriac, peeled

2 parsnips, peeled

2 raw beetroot, peeled

2 shallots, peeled

2 tsp chopped chives

3–4 tbsp citrus mayonnaise (from above)

To serve

1 large bunch of watercress, washed and trimmed

1 lemon, cut into 6 wedges

First make the citrus mayonnaise. Put the egg yolks, mustard, garlic, wine vinegar and citrus zests into a food processor and blend for 1 minute. With the motor running, very slowly add the olive oil through the funnel – the mayonnaise will emulsify and thicken. Season with salt and pepper to taste. Cover and refrigerate unless using straight away.

To make the salad, slice all the vegetables across into fine slices, then cut across the slices to give you julienne (matchsticks). Put the vegetable julienne into a bowl with the chopped chives and toss with some of the citrus mayonnaise to bind. Season with salt to taste.

Shortly before cooking, cut the monkfish into thumb-sized pieces and season with salt and pepper. Heat the oil in a deep-fryer to 200°C. Have the flour, eggs and breadcrumbs ready in 3 separate bowls. One at a time, pass the pieces of fish through the flour, then the egg and finally the breadcrumbs to coat evenly all over. Once coated, lay the pieces out on a tray.

When ready to serve, deep-fry the monkfish in the hot oil in batches for about 2 minutes until golden and crispy. Drain on kitchen paper and season with salt; keep hot while you cook the rest.

Place a neat mound of salad and some watercress on each serving plate. Divide the monkfish 'scampi' between the plates and add a dollop of citrus mayonnaise and a lemon wedge. Serve the rest of the mayonnaise in a pot on the side.

Monkfish with shellfish sauce and grilled leeks

Monkfish cooked on the bone over charcoal has got to be up there with the greatest flavours I have ever tasted. Mitch Tonks and Mat Prowse at The Seahorse in Devon showed me how they cooked it one day, when I was visiting them. It was possibly the best fish I've ever tasted. This dish is inspired by that day, with a twist of my own – the shellfish sauce that's been so faithful to me over the years.

Serves 4

4 monkfish tails on the bone, 300–400g each, trimmed of sinew and skin

12 baby leeks or spring onions, washed and trimmed

olive oil for cooking

2 baby gem lettuces, separated into leaves

Cornish sea salt and freshly ground black pepper

Shellfish sauce

750ml roast fish stock (page 222)

250ml shellfish stock (page 222)

5 ripe tomatoes, skinned, deseeded and chopped

5 tarragon sprigs

pinch of saffron strands

50g unsalted butter

To make the shellfish sauce, pour both stocks into a large saucepan and add the tomatoes, tarragon, saffron and butter. Bring to a simmer and let bubble until reduced to about 200ml. Tip the contents of the pan into a blender and blitz for 4 minutes. This will emulsify everything together, resulting in a velvety sauce. Taste for seasoning, adding salt and pepper as required. Allow to cool.

Add the leeks or spring onions to a pan of boiling salted water and cook for 2 minutes. Drain and immediately refresh in a bowl of iced water. Drain again and set aside.

If cooking outdoors, light the barbecue well ahead. Otherwise heat your grill to medium-high just before cooking. Season the monkfish with salt and pepper and drizzle over a little oil. Cook for 5–6 minutes on each side, until the fish starts to come away from the bone.

While the monkfish is cooking, season the leeks and barbecue or cook them on a hot griddle for 1 minute on each side to warm them through and give them a good colour. Gently heat up the shellfish sauce. Heat a little olive oil in a saucepan and lightly wilt down the baby gem lettuce.

To serve, divide the wilted lettuce between 4 warmed plates. Spoon the shellfish sauce on next and then top with the monkfish and leeks.

Rays & skate

You will come across skate on most UK fish restaurant menus at some point of the year, but I very much doubt it is skate, which has become scarce. It is more likely to be a ray of some sort. Members of the same family, both rays and skate are flat and cartilaginous and it is difficult to differentiate between them. However, rays give birth to live young ones whereas skates lay egg cases, known as mermaid's purses, which take 6 months to hatch into little skates. Most are landed on boats targeting flat fish, as they are mainly bottom-dwellers. The camouflage kings of the seabed, they lie buried in the sand, waiting to feed on small fish and crustaceans that come by.

Rays and skates are effortless to eat because the flesh slides easily from their cartilaginous framework once cooked. But unfortunately demand has led to sustainability issues with species of both fish. Currently the only rays we should be eating are the spotted, starry and cuckoo rays; all skates should be avoided. Once caught these fish are generally prepared on board – their 'wings' cut from the body and skinned, so it is difficult to tell what species you are buying. Avoid them in their breeding seasons: spring and early summer for spotted, from Christmas through spring for cuckoo, and autumn for starry ray.

Unlike other fish, skates and rays really do benefit from ageing a little before eating. They are perfect to eat 3 days after they've been caught. Before that their flesh is tough, a bit tasteless and has a slight aroma of urine, owing to the presence of urea, which protects them from the salt in the sea and prevents them from dehydrating. The urea is purged from the flesh naturally during those first 3 days after landing, leaving the flesh sweet and tender to eat. After 5 days, they develop a smell of ammonia, which obviously isn't nice either. A good fishmonger will sell them to you at the right stage for eating.

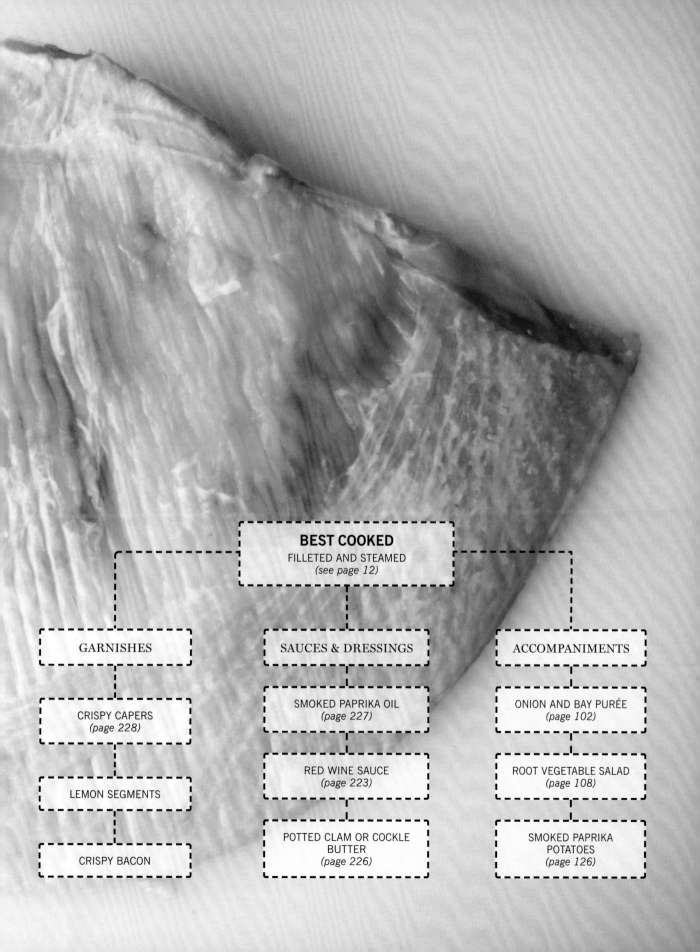

BEST COOKED
FILLETED AND STEAMED
(see page 12)

GARNISHES

SAUCES & DRESSINGS

ACCOMPANIMENTS

CRISPY CAPERS
(page 228)

SMOKED PAPRIKA OIL
(page 227)

ONION AND BAY PURÉE
(page 102)

LEMON SEGMENTS

RED WINE SAUCE
(page 223)

ROOT VEGETABLE SALAD
(page 108)

CRISPY BACON

POTTED CLAM OR COCKLE
BUTTER
(page 226)

SMOKED PAPRIKA
POTATOES
(page 126)

Peppered ray with tarragon, lemon and mustard brown butter

When I worked at Rick Stein's Seafood Restaurant in Padstow, skate with black butter was always on the menu. It was one of my favourite dishes to cook, and boy, did I cook a lot of them. This is my version of that dish. The tarragon and lemon work so well with the mustard and cracked pepper. You can change the citrus and herb if you wish, but I think this combination is perfect with fish.

Serves 4

4 ray or skate wings, about 300g each, trimmed and left on the bone

light rapeseed oil for cooking

2 tsp cracked black pepper

Tarragon, lemon and mustard brown butter

200g salted butter

100ml red wine

100ml red wine vinegar

4 tsp wholegrain mustard

2 shallots, peeled and chopped

2 garlic cloves, peeled and chopped

4 tsp chopped tarragon

1 lemon, peel and pith removed, segmented and finely chopped

Cornish sea salt and freshly ground black pepper

Heat your oven to 200°C/Gas 6. Lay the ray wings on a board and season with salt. Heat a large non-stick frying pan over a medium-high heat and add a little oil. Place the ray wings in the pan and cook for 2 minutes until the edges start to turn golden. (You may need to do this in batches.) Transfer the fish to an oiled large baking tray, turning the wings coloured side up. Sprinkle the cracked pepper over the surface and place in the oven for 6 minutes to finish cooking.

Meanwhile, to make the tarragon, lemon and mustard brown butter, clean the frying pan and return to a high heat. Add the butter to the pan and allow it to melt and turn golden brown. While it is melting, mix the wine and wine vinegar together. As soon as the butter is golden brown, add the wine mixture, taking care as it may spit! Remove the pan from the heat and add the mustard, shallots, garlic, tarragon and lemon. Give it a good stir.

Place the ray wings on warmed plates and pour the butter equally over them. Serve at once, with seasonal vegetables on the side.

Poached ray with leeks, lentils and sherry vinegar

Poaching ray this way really is a great way to cook it. All the moisture is retained within the flesh, which makes for perfect eating. Charred leeks, earthy lentils and sherry vinegar come together to complement the fish perfectly. If you want to do something a little different to the fish, then stuff it with herbs of your choice before rolling and poaching.

Serves 4

4 ray or skate wings, about 400g each, filleted and trimmed of sinew

100g caster sugar

100ml sherry vinegar

200g Puy or green lentils, rinsed

2 shallots, peeled and chopped

2 garlic cloves, peeled and chopped

16 baby leeks, washed and trimmed

50g unsalted butter

olive oil for cooking

1 bunch of spring onions, trimmed and sliced

2 tbsp chopped chives

Cornish sea salt and freshly ground black pepper

Lay a top side, thicker ray fillet on a large piece of cling film on your work surface. Season with salt and roll up into a sausage. Wrap tightly in the cling film and tie the ends tightly so it holds its shape. Repeat with the other larger fillets to give you 4 rolls. Refrigerate until ready to cook. (Keep the thinner fillets to coat in breadcrumbs and fry for lunch or a snack the next day.)

Dissolve the sugar in the sherry vinegar in a saucepan over a medium heat and bring to a simmer. Let bubble for 2 minutes and then set aside to cool.

Put the lentils in a saucepan with the shallots and garlic. Pour on cold water to cover and bring to a simmer over a medium heat. Skim, then simmer for about 7 minutes. Drain and spread out on a tray. While still hot, drizzle over some of the sherry vinegar reduction; this will be absorbed as the lentils cool. Refrigerate once cooled, unless using straight away.

To cook the leeks, lay them flat in a wide, shallow pan and add the butter and a sprinkling of salt. Cover with water and bring to a simmer over a medium heat. Cook for 3–4 minutes until soft on the outside, but still a little firm in the centre. Drain and spread out on a tray to cool.

To cook the fish, half-fill a wide, shallow pan with water and bring to a simmer. Add the film-wrapped ray rolls and poach for 6 minutes.

While the fish is cooking, place a large non-stick pan over a medium heat. When hot, add a drizzle of olive oil, then the leeks. Cook for 2 minutes until starting to colour, then flip them over, add the spring onions and cook for a further minute. Remove the leeks and keep warm. Add the lentils to the pan and heat though for 1 minute, then add 4 tbsp of the sherry vinegar reduction and the chopped chives. Taste for seasoning; keep warm.

Remove the cling film from the fish. Place a non-stick frying pan over a medium heat. When hot, add a little oil, then carefully place the ray rolls in the pan and cook for 2 minutes, turning carefully, until golden.

Divide the warm lentils and spring onions between 4 warmed plates. Place the leeks and fish on top. Finish with a drizzle of sherry reduction and serve.

ROUND WHITE FISH

Red mullet

As the seas around Britain have become warmer, red mullet have taken up residence. In the past, they would just visit for the summer when the water was warmer, but now commercial fisherman can usually rely on catching them right through the season. In reality this striking fish isn't a mullet at all, it's a member of the tropical goatfish family. It's a very sociable fish and swims with others, pecking at the mud and silt to find small crustaceans and worms.

Red mullet grow quickly and reach maturity when they're quite young, which is great from a sustainability angle. It means that you can enjoy them with a clear conscience, especially if they have been caught from inshore day boats using gill nets. The best time to ask your fishmonger for these amazing fish is between August and October; they should be avoided from May to July, which is the spawning season.

In my view, the finest way to experience red mullet is grilled whole until the skin crisps up and becomes almost like fish crackling, while the flesh within stays moist and juicy. And when red mullet are really fresh you can eat the livers, which are amazing chopped, pan-fried and spread on a piece of toast.

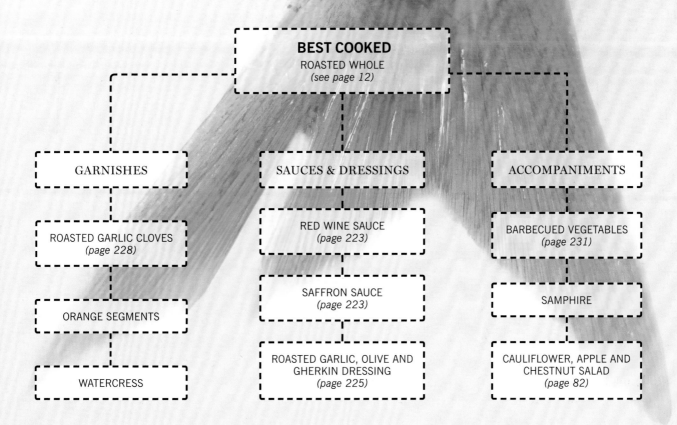

BEST COOKED
ROASTED WHOLE
(see page 12)

GARNISHES

SAUCES & DRESSINGS

ACCOMPANIMENTS

ROASTED GARLIC CLOVES
(page 228)

RED WINE SAUCE
(page 223)

BARBECUED VEGETABLES
(page 231)

ORANGE SEGMENTS

SAFFRON SAUCE
(page 223)

SAMPHIRE

WATERCRESS

ROASTED GARLIC, OLIVE AND
GHERKIN DRESSING
(page 225)

CAULIFLOWER, APPLE AND
CHESTNUT SALAD
(page 82)

Red mullet baked with rosemary and wild garlic

This is my favourite way to eat red mullet. To me, roasting any fish on the bone makes all the difference to the flavour. Traditionally, whole red mullet are cooked with their innards intact, but I prefer to gut the fish and cook the livers separately – seasoned nicely and wrapped in wild garlic to protect them. When wild garlic is out of season, simply fry the livers with a few whole garlic cloves to lend flavour.

Serves 4

4 red mullet, about 400g each, scaled, gutted (livers reserved)

8 wild garlic (ramson) leaves

4 rosemary stems

olive oil for cooking

100g butter

1 shallot, peeled and chopped

50ml cider

Cornish sea salt and freshly ground black pepper

Heat your oven to 200°C/Gas 6 and put a roasting tray inside to heat up. Wash the red mullet livers, pat dry and season with salt and pepper. Wrap them in the wild garlic leaves.

Score the fish diagonally, making 3 or 4 slashes on each side and insert little sprigs of rosemary into the slashes. Season the fish all over with salt and pepper. Add a drizzle of oil to the roasting tray. Add the remaining rosemary to the tray and place the fish on top, side by side. Dot with the butter and bake for 8–10 minutes.

Meanwhile, heat a non-stick frying pan, then add a drizzle of oil. When it is hot, add the wrapped fish livers and cook for 1 minute. Flip the liver parcels over, add the shallot and cider to the pan and cook for 1 minute. Remove the wrapped livers and set aside with the fish.

Add a few spoonfuls of the fish cooking juices to the cider and shallots in the pan and heat, stirring to combine and make a dressing.

Place the red mullet and wrapped livers on warmed plates. Pour over the dressing and serve at once, with buttery mashed potatoes.

Red mullet with saffron, orange oil and spring onion barley

When we get smaller red mullet, I like to butterfly them as it's a great way to prepare and serve these beautiful fish. To me, the taste of red mullet has notes of saffron and orange zest, so it makes sense to use those flavours in the barley and dressing.

Serves 4

4 red mullet, 200–300g each, scaled, gutted and butterflied (see page 250)

olive oil for cooking

50g unsalted butter

8 spring onions, trimmed and finely sliced, white and dark green part kept separate

2 garlic cloves, peeled and finely chopped

100g pearl barley

about 200ml vegetable stock (page 222)

1 tsp saffron strands

200g spinach, washed and trimmed

2 tsp chopped dill, plus extra fronds to garnish

50g Parmesan, grated

orange oil (page 227)

Cornish sea salt and freshly ground black pepper

Heat a large saucepan over a medium heat and add a drizzle of olive oil and the butter. When hot, add the white spring onion and garlic to the pan. Cook, stirring, for 1 minute, then add the pearl barley, stir and cook for another minute.

Pour in the vegetable stock and add the saffron. Bring to the boil and simmer for about 20 minutes until the barley is cooked but retaining a bite, and the liquid is almost completely absorbed. Taste the barley; if it is still a little undercooked, add a little more stock and continue to simmer until tender.

Now add the green spring onion, spinach and dill, and cook for 1 minute. Stir in the Parmesan and then check the seasoning, adding salt and pepper to taste. Keep warm.

To cook the fish, heat your grill to medium and oil and season the grill tray. Place the fish skin side up on the grill tray. Cook under the grill for 4 minutes or until the fish is just cooked through.

Spoon the barley onto 4 warmed plates and place the red mullet on top. Add 4 tbsp orange oil to the grill tray and stir to mix with the cooking juices and create a little dressing. Drizzle over and around the fish, scatter over some dill fronds and serve at once.

Sea bass

When you prepare a sea bass from scratch you will, at some point, stab yourself with one of its many sharp spines. It's inevitable. Now imagine you come up against this fish in the water. Sea bass is the ultimate fighting and hunting machine, and it's a bully. Whether small and moving around in a group, or a large adult hunting alone, sea bass are deadly predators. Personally I can forgive them, because of what lies beneath those sharp spines and scales…

With a beautiful flavour and succulent, part oily, part creamy, flaky flesh, sea bass is as good as it gets. It is excellent cooked whole or as fillets and served very simply, but it is also robust enough to take a strong shellfish sauce or even a red wine one.

As the demand for this amazing fish has increased over the last 30 years, so the price has escalated. It is certainly not the cheap alternative to cod that it once was. Trawlers have taken their toll, but a lot of the sea bass landed in the Southwest is now line caught and targeted as such – a more sustainable option. Bass do take a while to get to maturity, about 5 years, so it is particularly important to avoid them altogether in spring and early summer when they are breeding. They can live to a ripe old age of 25. I like to get sea bass in the 1.5–2kg size range and never buy one measuring less than 36cm. Sometimes we get larger fish and then I'm most likely to cook them whole. The best time to eat sea bass is towards the end of the summer.

BEST COOKED
FILLETED AND GRILLED
OR ROASTED WHOLE
(see page 12)

GARNISHES

RED WINE SHALLOTS
(page 231)

WILD FENNEL

GOOSEBERRY JAM
(page 154)

SAUCES & DRESSINGS

PICCALILLI SAUCE
(page 224)

SHELLFISH SAUCE
(page 223)

BEETROOT DRESSING
(page 158)

ACCOMPANIMENTS

SPICED PICKLED
VEGETABLES
(page 232)

SUMMER VEGETABLE
NAGE
(page 60)

POTATO, GARLIC AND
HERB DUMPLINGS
(page 230)

Baked sea bass with soused vegetables and smoked paprika potatoes

This is a great way to cook bigger sea bass that you may be able to get hold of once in a while. It is so easy to take the fillets off a cooked whole bass, so do give it a go. The accompanying soused vegetables and smoked paprika potatoes are the perfect foil for this part oily fish.

Serves 4

1 sea bass, at least 2kg, fins and spines removed, scaled and gutted

100ml olive oil

4 shallots, peeled and halved

2 large carrots, sliced

2 red peppers, cored, deseeded and cut into broad strips

2 fennel bulbs, trimmed, halved and sliced

8 spring onions, trimmed

100ml white wine

100ml white wine vinegar

100g caster sugar

3 tsp chopped dill

3 tsp chopped tarragon

Cornish sea salt and freshly ground black pepper

Smoked paprika potatoes

200g new potatoes, washed

1 tsp smoked paprika

Heat your oven to 220°C/Gas 7. In a roasting tray or dish big enough to take the bass, lay the shallots, carrots, red peppers, fennel and spring onions out to form a trellis. Lightly oil the sea bass with a little of the olive oil, season with salt and pepper all over and lay on top of the vegetables. Drizzle some more of the olive oil over the vegetables. Bake in the oven for 20 minutes.

Meanwhile, for the smoked paprika potatoes, cook the new potatoes in a pan of boiling salted water until tender. Drain and leave until cool enough to handle, then cut in half; set aside.

Mix the wine, wine vinegar, sugar and all but a drizzle of the remaining olive oil together. Pour this mixture evenly over the vegetables and sea bass in the roasting tray and return to the oven for a further 10 minutes.

While the fish is cooking, place a non-stick pan over a medium heat and add a drizzle of olive oil. When hot, add the cooked potatoes and smoked paprika and cook for 5 minutes, stirring every minute to colour and crisp evenly. Season with salt and pepper to taste. Drain the potatoes on kitchen paper, then set aside in a warm bowl.

Once the fish is cooked, remove the roasting tray from the oven and carefully transfer the whole bass and vegetables to a warmed serving platter, draining off excess liquor. Add the smoked paprika potatoes and scatter over the chopped herbs to serve. Alternatively you can serve the fish and vegetables directly from the roasting tray or dish, adding the potatoes and herbs.

Grilled sea bass, smoked mackerel pâté and pickled cucumber

Fillets of sea bass grilled to the point of the skin blistering and becoming crispy are amazing. Carefully balancing the other flavours and textures in this dish ensures they don't interfere with the simplicity of the grilled fish. The smoked mackerel pâté is delicious – try it on toast or in a sandwich.

Serves 4

4 filleted sea bass portions, from a 1.5kg fish, pin-boned

olive oil for cooking

Cornish sea salt and freshly ground black pepper

Pickled cucumber

1 cucumber

50ml white wine

50ml white wine vinegar

50g caster sugar

2 shallots, peeled and finely chopped

1 garlic clove, peeled and finely chopped

50ml water

2 tsp chopped dill (stalks reserved), plus extra sprigs to garnish

2 tsp chopped chives

Smoked mackerel pâté

300g smoked mackerel fillet, skinned and pin-boned

juice of 1 lemon

100g natural yoghurt

100g cream cheese

To finish (optional)

lemon oil (page 227)

To prepare the pickled cucumber, halve the cucumber lengthways and scoop out the seeds with a spoon. Cut lengthways into long 5mm thick slices and place in a bowl. For the pickling liquor, put the wine, wine vinegar, sugar, shallots, garlic and water into a pan and bring to the boil. Add a pinch of salt and the dill stalks, then pour the boiling liquid over the cucumber. Leave to cool. Discard the dill stalks and add the chopped dill and chives.

To make the pâté, put the smoked mackerel and most of the lemon juice into a food processor and blend for 1 minute, scraping down the sides of the bowl once or twice. Add the yoghurt and cream cheese and blend for 2 minutes until well combined. Taste for seasoning and adjust with salt, pepper and a little more lemon juice if needed. Scoop into a dish, cover and chill until required.

To cook the fish, heat your grill to medium and oil the grill tray. Season the bass with salt and pepper and drizzle over a little olive oil. Lay the fillets, skin side up, on the oiled tray and place under the grill. Cook for 5 minutes or until the skin starts to colour and crisp.

Place the bass fillets on warmed plates. Add a portion of pickled cucumber and top with a generous spoonful of smoked mackerel. Garnish with dill sprigs and finish with a drizzle of lemon oil if you wish.

Sea bass with crab mayonnaise, roasted fennel and orange

Sea bass and crab are natural partners, like lamb and rosemary. From an oriental-style to an Italian dish, these great ingredients of the ocean seem to come together in so many cuisines.

Serves 4

4 filleted sea bass portions, about 200g each

1 live brown crab, about 1kg, placed in the freezer 1 hour before cooking (see page 256)

2 fennel bulbs, trimmed and halved

light rapeseed oil for cooking

1 orange, peel and pith removed, segmented and diced

olive oil to drizzle

Cornish sea salt and freshly ground black pepper

Mayonnaise and sauce

2 egg yolks

finely grated zest and juice of 1 lemon

300ml light olive oil

2 tbsp chopped tarragon

50ml double cream

100ml crab stock (page 222)

Bring a large pan of water to the boil (big enough to submerge the crab). Season the water liberally with sea salt to make it as salty as seawater (see page 256). When the water comes to a rolling boil, lower the crab into it and cook for 15 minutes.

Carefully lift the crab out of the water, place on a board and leave until cool enough to handle. Prepare and extract the meat from the crab (as described on page 256). Save the shell for the stock. Blend the brown crab meat in a food processor until smooth and save for the crab mayonnaise. Pick through the white meat removing any shell and cartilage; keep cool.

For the mayonnaise, whisk the egg yolks, lemon juice and zest in a bowl and slowly add the oil drop by drop to begin with, then in a steady stream, whisking constantly. Mix half of this into the white crab meat with 2 tbsp brown meat, the chopped tarragon and salt and pepper to taste. Keep cool.

For the sauce, whisk the cream into the rest of the mayonnaise and thin down with the crab stock. Keep cool until serving.

Heat your oven to 200°C/Gas 6. Cut each fennel half into 6 or 8 wedges. Heat a non-stick frying pan over a medium heat and add a drizzle of oil. When hot, add the fennel wedges and cook for 2 minutes on each side until golden. Season with salt and pepper and transfer the fennel to an oven tray. Place in the oven for 4 minutes.

Meanwhile, heat an ovenproof non-stick frying pan and add a drizzle of oil. When hot, place the fish, skin side down, in the pan and season with salt. Cook until the skin starts to turn golden, then transfer to the oven to cook for 4 minutes.

When ready, take out the fennel; keep warm. Remove the fish and flip it over; it will finish cooking in the heat of the pan. Warm the crab sauce.

Spoon the crab mayonnaise into the centre of 4 warmed plates, top with the fish and place the fennel alongside. Spoon the crab sauce around the fish. Finish with the orange pieces and a drizzle of olive oil. Serve at once.

Whiting

Whiting really hasn't got a great reputation for flavour. It has long been regarded as a somewhat bland fish, but I see it differently. Subtle tasting it may be, but it is a highly versatile fish that can be matched with a wide variety of flavours – from the tastiest of shellfish sauces to the most delicate of salads. The one slight downside is that – like mackerel – whiting must be eaten very fresh, as it deteriorates rapidly once landed.

A member of the cod family, whiting is just as lazy and greedy as its more popular cousin, although it is less of a loner, preferring to swim in big shoals. Whiting swim mainly inshore and love big sandy stretches of seabed where they can pick off shrimps, crab and worms. This makes them pretty easy to catch. They are also quite sustainable and give us a different fish option at a time of the year when there is not much else about – from November to February. They should be avoided from March to July when they are spawning.

Most of the whiting you'll find in fishmongers weigh around 1.5kg, and more often than not they are sold as fillets. Occasionally you will come across larger whiting, around 2.5–3kg, which are ideal for cooking and serving whole.

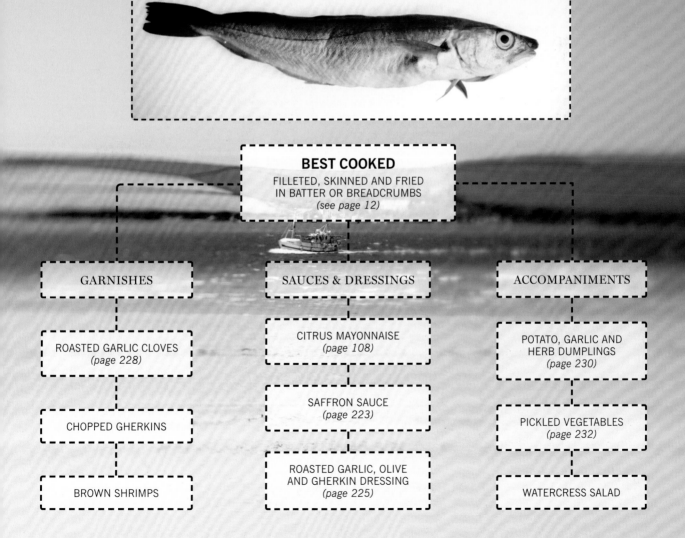

BEST COOKED
FILLETED, SKINNED AND FRIED IN BATTER OR BREADCRUMBS
(see page 12)

GARNISHES

ROASTED GARLIC CLOVES
(page 228)

CHOPPED GHERKINS

BROWN SHRIMPS

SAUCES & DRESSINGS

CITRUS MAYONNAISE
(page 108)

SAFFRON SAUCE
(page 223)

ROASTED GARLIC, OLIVE AND GHERKIN DRESSING
(page 225)

ACCOMPANIMENTS

POTATO, GARLIC AND HERB DUMPLINGS
(page 230)

PICKLED VEGETABLES
(page 232)

WATERCRESS SALAD

Whiting with grape dressing and roast garlic and potato purée

On a chilly autumn evening when you feel the need for comfort food, this dish will do the trick. Buttery mashed potatoes and a salty, sweet dressing topped with a lovely flaky fresh fillet of roasted whiting... warming and deeply satisfying.

Serves 4

4 thick whiting fillets (skin on), about 200g each, or 8 small fillets, pin-boned and halved

olive oil for cooking

Cornish sea salt and freshly ground black pepper

Roast garlic and potato purée

800g medium-large potatoes, washed

1 garlic bulb

200ml milk

200ml double cream

4 tsp chopped flat-leaf parsley

Grape dressing

150g unsalted butter

1 shallot, peeled and chopped

1 garlic clove, peeled and finely chopped

100ml Noilly Prat or other dry vermouth

20 grapes, halved and deseeded

2 tsp chopped chervil

To finish

8 roasted garlic cloves, unpeeled (see right)

To make the roast garlic and potato purée, heat your oven to 200°C/Gas 6. Place the whole potatoes on an oven tray and bake for 30 minutes, then turn over and cook for a further 20 minutes. Place the garlic bulb on a piece of foil, sprinkle with 1 tsp salt and drizzle with a little olive oil, then wrap up in the foil. Place the foil parcel and the garlic cloves for the garnish on the tray alongside the potatoes and bake for a further 20 minutes. Reserve the roasted individual garlic cloves for the garnish.

Working quite quickly, halve the potatoes and scoop out the flesh into a bowl. Unwrap the roasted garlic bulb, then separate and peel the cloves. Pass the potato and garlic through a potato ricer into a bowl, or mash them together smoothly. Heat the milk and cream together and slowly incorporate into the potato mix until you have the consistency you like. Season with salt and pepper to taste and add the chopped parsley. Cover and keep hot.

To make the grape dressing, melt the butter in a pan over a medium heat and heat until it turns nut brown, then take off the heat. Place another pan over a medium heat and add a drizzle of oil. When hot, add the chopped shallot and garlic and cook for 1 minute, without colouring. Now add the vermouth and reduce down to about 2 tbsp. Add the grapes and remove from the heat.

To cook the fish, heat an ovenproof non-stick frying pan over a medium heat. When hot, drizzle in some oil, then add the fish fillets, skin side down. Season with salt and cook for 2 minutes until the edges turn golden, then place the pan in the oven for 3 minutes. Meanwhile, add 8 tbsp of the brown butter to the grape mixture and warm through; do not boil. As you take the fish from the oven, flip it over; it will finish cooking with the heat from the pan as you serve.

Spoon the roast garlic and potato purée onto 4 warmed plates. Using a fish slice, carefully place the fish skin side up on top. Add the chopped chervil to the dressing and season to taste, then divide between the plates. Finish with the roasted garlic cloves.

Poached whiting, summer vegetable broth and chervil dumplings

A light dish, bursting with summer flavours, this recipe works perfectly with the smaller whiting fillets that are more readily available. Poaching the fish in this way is a wonderful way of cooking it, as none of the flavour is lost – it simply enhances the broth.

Serves 4

4 whiting fillets, about 300g each, skinned, trimmed, cut in half and pin-boned

light rapeseed oil for cooking

Cornish sea salt and freshly ground black pepper

Vegetable broth

olive oil for cooking

2 shallots, peeled and diced

2 garlic cloves, peeled and finely chopped

1 fennel bulb, trimmed and diced

4 celery sticks, washed, peeled and diced

200ml vegetable stock (page 222)

200ml roast fish stock (page 222)

8 Swiss chard stems, washed

100g green beans, trimmed and sliced into 1cm pieces

2 courgettes, trimmed and diced

4 tomatoes, skinned, deseeded and chopped

100ml double cream

50g unsalted butter

4 tsp chopped chervil, plus extra sprigs to finish

To serve

potato, garlic and herb dumplings (page 230)

Have the dumplings prepared and ready to finish and serve.

For the broth, heat a large saucepan over a medium heat, then add a good drizzle of olive oil. When hot, add the shallots, garlic, fennel and celery and sweat for 2 minutes without colouring, stirring all the time. Pour in both stocks and bring up to a simmer. Let simmer for 6 minutes. Meanwhile, separate the chard leaves from their stalks. Finely dice the stalks and shred the leaves. Add to the broth with the green beans, courgettes and tomatoes. Simmer gently for 5 minutes.

Meanwhile, season the portions of whiting with salt and pepper. Heat a non-stick frying pan and add a drizzle of oil. When hot, add the dumplings and cook, turning, for 2–3 minutes until golden brown. Drain on kitchen paper and keep warm.

Add the whiting fillets to the simmering broth and turn off the heat. Cover and allow the heat of the broth to cook the fish for 4 minutes.

Divide the dumplings between 4 warmed shallow bowls. Carefully remove the whiting from the broth with a spatula and place in the bowls. Add the cream and butter to the broth and quickly bring back to a simmer. Now add the chopped chervil. Ladle the broth and vegetables over and around the fish. Finish with chervil sprigs and serve.

Oily fish

Sardine & herring

Sardine or pilchard, which should it be? In fact these are the same fish, but it's the age and size that gives us the correct name. After 2 years a sardine becomes a pilchard and can go on to live well into double figures if it avoids its many predators. Traditionally caught using drift nets, stocks of sardines and pilchards are in a healthy state so you can eat them freely. Enjoy them in the summer and through until early winter, before they swim south to warmer waters. Rich in omega-3 fatty acids, these are very healthy fish and one of our finest to eat. As an added bonus, the bones in sardines are so small that you can eat them too. My favourite way to eat sardines is straight off the barbecue; they are also lovely cured and pickled.

Herring is another fish that we can feel good about eating. This oil-rich small fish is delicious, versatile and pretty sustainable. In my opinion it must be eaten very fresh, ideally as soon as it's landed. Herring are also great preserved or smoked, most famously pickled as rollmops or smoked as kippers. I'm also partial to the creamy roe or 'milts' on toast. Fresh herrings can be eaten all year and are at their best through the autumn. Herring swim in large shoals of similar age and spawn in shallow waters on an annual cycle. When you see or catch a herring you'll understand the nickname 'silver darling'. They sparkle and shimmer in the water in a remarkable way.

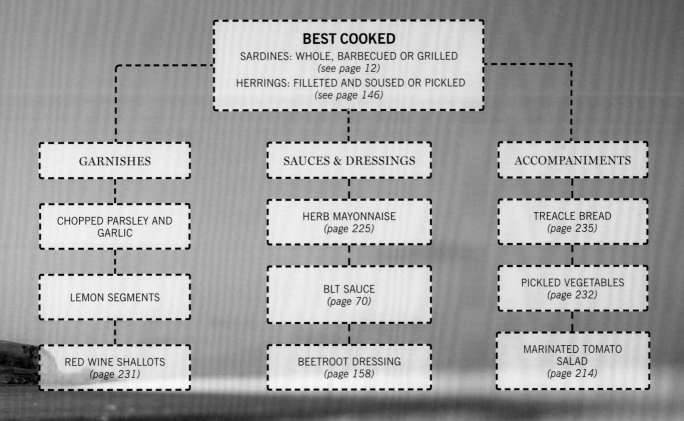

BEST COOKED
SARDINES: WHOLE, BARBECUED OR GRILLED
(see page 12)
HERRINGS: FILLETED AND SOUSED OR PICKLED
(see page 146)

GARNISHES

SAUCES & DRESSINGS

ACCOMPANIMENTS

CHOPPED PARSLEY AND GARLIC

HERB MAYONNAISE
(page 225)

TREACLE BREAD
(page 235)

LEMON SEGMENTS

BLT SAUCE
(page 70)

PICKLED VEGETABLES
(page 232)

RED WINE SHALLOTS
(page 231)

BEETROOT DRESSING
(page 158)

MARINATED TOMATO SALAD
(page 214)

Sardine and tomato soup with basil oil

I love oily sardines with just-picked, summery tomatoes, and bringing them together in a light, flavoursome soup works a treat. Finish with a drizzle of basil oil for a Mediterranean touch.

Serves 4 generously

1kg sardines, scaled, gutted and washed, plus an extra 4 butterflied sardines (see page 250) to serve

100ml olive oil

2 onions, peeled and chopped

1 large fennel bulb, trimmed and chopped

2 leeks (white and pale green part only), washed and chopped

6 garlic cloves, peeled and chopped

1 rosemary sprig

2 bay leaves

30 basil leaves

500g ripe, flavourful plum tomatoes, halved and chopped

1 litre water

To serve

basil oil (page 227)

Heat a large saucepan over a medium heat, then add half the olive oil. When the oil is hot, add the onions, fennel, leeks, garlic, rosemary, bay leaves and basil and cook for 5 minutes, stirring all the time. Add the tomatoes and cook for a further 5 minutes, then add the water and simmer for 30 minutes.

While the soup base is simmering, heat a large non-stick frying pan over a medium heat and add a drizzle of olive oil. When the oil is hot, add as many sardines as you can fit into the pan in a single layer and cook until blistered and golden, about 4 minutes. Flip them over and cook for another 4 minutes. Repeat, if necessary, to cook the rest of the sardines, adding them to the soup pan as they are cooked.

Tip the contents of the soup pan into a food processor or blender, or use a hand-held stick blender to blitz the soup until it is as smooth as you can possibly get it. Strain through a sieve into a clean saucepan and set aside.

When you are ready to serve, place a non-stick frying pan over a medium heat. When the pan is hot, add a drizzle of oil and lay the butterflied sardine fillets in the pan, skin side down. Cook, without moving, for 2 minutes, then take the pan off the heat and flip the sardine fillets over; they will finish cooking in the residual heat.

Meanwhile, gently reheat the soup, taste for seasoning and adjust as necessary. Divide the soup between warmed bowls and place a butterflied sardine on top of each portion. Drizzle with some basil oil and serve.

Barbecued sardines with brown bread salad and salad cream

To me, there is something very British and nostalgic about this dish. It's probably more to do with the salad cream than anything else. Mayonnaise wasn't on offer when I was a child; it was always salad cream on the table. We didn't have sardines this way either; they came from a tin, which incidentally, is still fine with me today!

Serves 4

4 large or 8 small sardines, scaled, gutted, washed and butterflied (see page 250)

olive oil for cooking and to drizzle

8 slices of wholemeal or granary bread

1 garlic clove, halved

Cornish sea salt and freshly ground black pepper

Salad

1 cucumber

12 cherry tomatoes

12 radishes

2 tsp chopped dill

2 tsp chopped capers

2 tsp chopped gherkins

Salad cream

2 egg yolks

2 tsp English mustard

2 tsp caster sugar

2 tbsp lemon juice

100ml rapeseed oil

150ml double cream

Light your barbecue well ahead.

For the salad, peel the cucumber, halve lengthways and slice. Halve the tomatoes and thinly slice the radishes. Put them all in a bowl and add the dill, capers and gherkins. Toss together and leave to one side.

To make the salad cream, put the egg yolks, mustard, sugar and lemon juice into a bowl and whisk together for 1 minute, then gradually add the oil, drop by drop to begin with, then in a steady stream, until it is all incorporated. To finish, slowly whisk in the cream and season with salt to taste. Refrigerate until required.

When the barbecue coals are white hot, oil the sardines and season them all over with salt and pepper. Lay them skin side down on the barbecue and cook for 3–4 minutes, then flip the fish over onto the other side and barbecue for another minute or until cooked. Carefully transfer the sardines to a warmed platter and rest for 1 minute.

Toast the slices of bread on the barbecue, colouring them well on both sides. Drizzle with some olive oil and rub with the cut garlic clove. Cut or break 4 slices into pieces and toss with the salad, dressing it with a little of the salad cream.

Place the other 4 slices of toast on individual plates. Add the salad, sardines and a generous dollop of salad cream.

Pickled herrings with cucumber and dill

This prepare-ahead dish takes the stress out of a dinner or lunch party starter, leaving you free to enjoy your time with your guests. It works well with any oily fish. I like to serve it on a nice, big platter as a centrepiece for a party.

Serves 4

4 herrings, scaled, gutted and filleted

1 tsp white peppercorns

2 tsp fennel seeds

2 bay leaves

2 shallots, peeled and finely sliced

2 garlic cloves, peeled and crushed

250ml cider vinegar

100g caster sugar

100ml lemon oil (page 227)

2 tbsp chopped dill

1 cucumber

Cornish sea salt

Lay the herring fillets in a dish large enough to hold them side by side immersed in the pickling liquor.

Put the peppercorns, fennel seeds, bay leaves, shallots, garlic, cider vinegar and sugar into a pan and bring to a simmer. Simmer for 2 minutes, then add 2 tsp salt. Remove from the heat and leave to cool to room temperature.

Pour the cooled liquor and all the flavourings over the herrings and cover the fish closely with cling film to keep them submerged. Leave the fish to marinate in the fridge for 24 hours before eating.

Take the dish out of the fridge at least an hour before serving to allow the fish to return to room temperature. To serve, strain 50ml of the cooking liquor and mix with the lemon oil and chopped dill. Halve and deseed the cucumber, then dice or slice as you prefer and add to the dressing. Season with salt to taste.

Lay the herring fillets on a serving platter, scatter over the cucumber and drizzle with the dressing. Serve with a simple leafy salad and crusty bread.

Mackerel

Mackerel is, without doubt, my favourite fish. I find it fantastically versatile and love nothing more than catching, cooking and eating it. Beautiful to look at and impressive in the sea, mackerel is an amazing creature. Basically a speed machine, it zooms through the water at a great pace in very large shoals hunting down small fry during the summer. Then, when winter comes, it's off to the deep to almost hibernate and wait until things warm up again. Mackerel is a mature fish at about 3 years, but during its first and second years it increases in size rapidly and piles on weight. It is best to avoid the fish during the spring, which is the spawning season.

Freshness is critical with mackerel. To appreciate this fish at its best, you really need to cook and eat it within a few hours of it being caught – ideally simply grilled or barbecued. To me, a freshly caught mackerel screams out to be cooked on a beach over coals the moment it is landed, and eaten there and then. If any mackerel has been around for a couple of days I would opt to cure and smoke it instead. Mackerel is amazingly good for you, particularly as it is packed with beneficial omega-3 fatty acids.

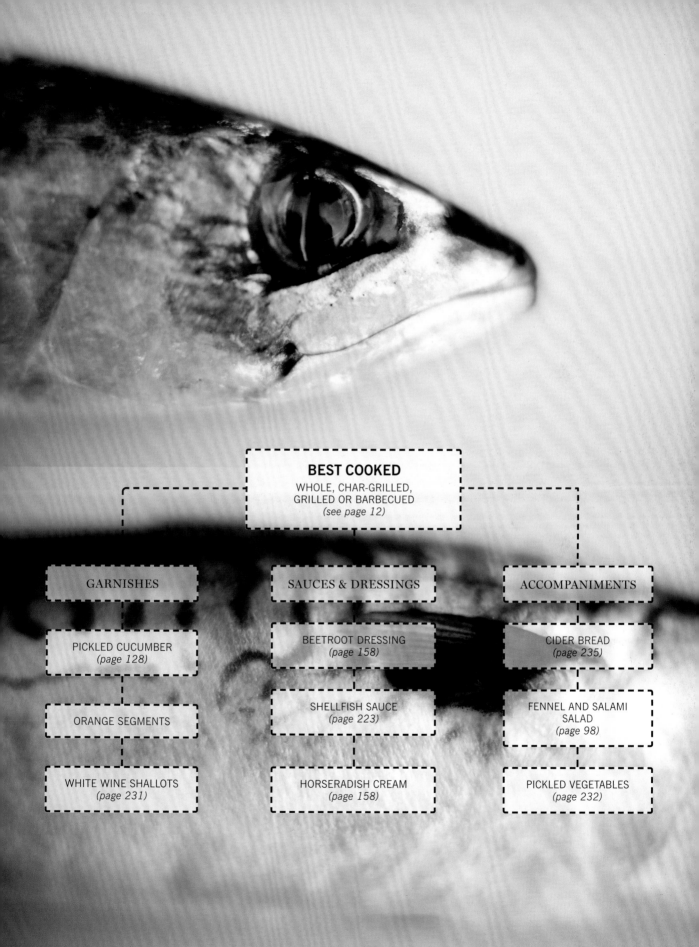

BEST COOKED
WHOLE, CHAR-GRILLED,
GRILLED OR BARBECUED
(see page 12)

GARNISHES

SAUCES & DRESSINGS

ACCOMPANIMENTS

PICKLED CUCUMBER
(page 128)

BEETROOT DRESSING
(page 158)

CIDER BREAD
(page 235)

ORANGE SEGMENTS

SHELLFISH SAUCE
(page 223)

FENNEL AND SALAMI
SALAD
(page 98)

WHITE WINE SHALLOTS
(page 231)

HORSERADISH CREAM
(page 158)

PICKLED VEGETABLES
(page 232)

Barbecued mackerel with beetroot and apple salad

Early beetroot appear as the first mackerel of the year are caught, so it makes sense to serve them together. The charred skin and moist, rich mackerel flesh marry perfectly with beetroot – and apple brings a crisp, sharp taste to cut the richness. When barbecuing fish make sure your coals are at the white hot stage and oil your fish before placing it on the hot grid, but not too much or your fish will be engulfed in flames and burn.

Serves 4

4 large or 8 small mackerel, gutted

light rapeseed oil for cooking

Cornish sea salt and freshly ground black pepper

Beetroot and apple salad

4 raw beetroot, washed and peeled

4 Granny Smith apples

50ml white wine vinegar

2 shallots, peeled and finely sliced

3 pickled walnuts, chopped (optional)

2 tsp chopped chives

4 tbsp mayonnaise (page 225)

To serve

1 lemon, cut into wedges

1 large baguette, sliced

To make the beetroot and apple salad, slice the beetroot across into fine slices, then cut across the slices to give you julienne (matchsticks). Peel and core the apples and similarly cut into julienne. Toss the apples and beetroot in a bowl with the wine vinegar, shallots, pickled walnuts if using, and chives. Add the mayonnaise and mix well. Taste for seasoning and add salt and pepper as required.

Light your barbecue well in advance and make sure the grid is very hot. Wash the mackerel and pat dry with kitchen paper. Oil the fish and season all over with salt and pepper. Place the fish on the barbecue grid and cook, without moving, for 5 minutes. Now turn the fish over. (If it has stuck then leave it for another minute before turning.) Barbecue for 4 minutes on the other side until the flesh inside the cavity is opaque all the way through.

Carefully lift the fish from the barbecue onto plates. Serve straight away, with the beetroot and apple salad and lemon wedges. Accompany with plenty of bread for mopping up the juices.

Mackerel on red pepper marmalade tart with smoked paprika mayonnaise

This dish was so popular on our menu that I decided to take it off, because we didn't sell anything else! Instead I turned it into a little snack to offer guests with drinks as they arrived, and everyone was happy. The oily mackerel and red pepper work brilliantly together and the paprika lends a smoky, spicy note.

Serves 4 as a starter

2 large or 4 small mackerel, filleted, trimmed and pin-boned

Red pepper marmalade tarts

6 red peppers

2 red onions, peeled and sliced

4 garlic cloves, peeled and chopped

100ml balsamic vinegar

50ml red wine vinegar

2 thyme sprigs, leaves picked and chopped

olive oil for cooking

100g caster sugar

200g good-quality ready-made puff pastry

Cornish sea salt and freshly ground black pepper

Smoked paprika mayonnaise

2 egg yolks

finely grated zest and juice of 1 lemon

200ml smoked paprika oil (page 227)

To serve

16 pickled baby onions in red wine (page 232), drained and halved

100g mixed salad leaves

Heat your oven to 200°C/Gas 6. For the red pepper marmalade, roast the red peppers on a roasting tray for 30 minutes. Transfer to a bowl, cover with cling film and leave to cool; the trapped steam will help to lift the skins. Meanwhile, put the red onions, garlic, both vinegars and the thyme into a pan and bring to a simmer. Let bubble over a medium heat until the liquid has reduced right down, almost to nothing; don't let the onions burn. Turn the oven down to 180°C/Gas 4.

Peel the skins from the peppers, then halve, core, deseed and slice them thinly. Heat a large non-stick frying pan over a medium heat. When hot, add a drizzle of oil and the peppers and sugar. Cook for 2 minutes, then add the red onion mixture and cook until the juice has reduced right down, almost to nothing. Taste and season the marmalade, then allow to cool and chill.

For the smoked paprika mayonnaise, put the egg yolks and lemon zest and juice into a bowl and whisk together for 1 minute. Add the oil, drop by drop to begin with, then in a steady stream, whisking constantly, until the mixture is emulsified and thick. Season with a little salt. Refrigerate until needed.

On a floured surface, roll out the pastry to the thickness of a £1 coin and prick all over with a fork. Cut out four 5cm circles and place on a lined baking sheet. Spread the red pepper marmalade evenly over the pastry circles, but not too thickly. Bake for 10 minutes, then turn the tarts over carefully and bake for a further 5 minutes. Cool on a wire rack.

To cook the mackerel, oil a non-stick frying pan and place the fish, skin side down, in the pan. Cook over a medium heat for 3 minutes until the skin is crispy, then flip over and remove from the heat; the fish will finish cooking in the residual heat.

To serve, add the pickled baby onions to the mackerel pan to warm through. Put a blob of paprika mayonnaise in the middle of each serving plate and place a red pepper tart on top. Arrange a few mixed leaves and the pickled onion halves on each plate, adding a few blobs of paprika mayonnaise. Lay the mackerel fillets on the tart and drizzle over any juices from the pan.

Cured mackerel and gooseberry jam roll

This unusual recipe was invented as an original way to use up leftover fresh mackerel, but you could use good-quality smoked fish instead and omit the curing stage. The acidity of the gooseberry cuts the richness of the mackerel perfectly. It's a great canapé to serve at a party, or to enjoy simply as a snack.

Serves 6 as a starter

2 mackerel, filleted, skinned and pin-boned

50g sea salt

1 tsp smoked paprika

25g caster sugar

50g cream cheese

25ml natural yoghurt

juice of ¼ lemon

Cornish sea salt and freshly ground black pepper

Gooseberry jam

light rapeseed oil for cooking

1 small shallot, peeled and chopped

100g gooseberries, topped and tailed

25g caster sugar

Savoury sponge

30g unsalted butter, plus extra to grease

45g plain flour

200ml hot milk

3 large eggs, separated

1 tsp chopped parsley

25g Parmesan, grated

Lay the mackerel fillets on a tray. Mix together the 50g salt, smoked paprika and sugar and sprinkle evenly over the fillets. Wrap in cling film or cover and chill for 2 hours.

Wash off the salt mixture and pat the mackerel dry. Heat your oven to 160°C/Gas 3. Lay the mackerel on an oiled baking tray and place in the oven for 2 minutes; it should be a little undercooked. Allow to cool down.

Put the cooled mackerel in a food processor with the cream cheese, yoghurt and lemon juice and pulse until evenly combined. Taste the mixture and season with salt and pepper if required. Cover and refrigerate.

To make the gooseberry jam, place a saucepan over a medium heat and add a little oil. When hot, add the shallot and gooseberries. Cook until the berries start to collapse, then add the sugar and season with salt and pepper. Cook for 1 minute or until most of the liquid has evaporated. Tip the mixture into a food processor and blend until smooth. Transfer to a bowl, cover and chill.

For the sponge, line a large baking tray with silicone paper and butter the paper. Melt the butter in a saucepan, stir in the flour and cook, stirring, over a medium heat for 2–3 minutes. Off the heat, add the milk, bit by bit, stirring all the time. Cook, stirring, for 3 more minutes, then remove from the heat.

In a clean bowl, whisk the egg whites until they form firm peaks. Stir the egg yolks into the cooked mixture, then carefully fold in the egg whites. Season with salt and pepper and fold in the chopped parsley. Spread the mixture evenly on the prepared tray and sprinkle over the Parmesan. Bake for 10 minutes until golden and springy to the touch. Leave on the tray for 10 minutes, then transfer to a wire rack to cool.

When the sponge is cold, spread with the mackerel mixture, followed by a layer of gooseberry jam. Roll up from a long side into a large roll and then wrap tightly in cling film and chill for 1 hour. To serve, slice the roll and warm it though in the oven for 3–4 minutes. Accompany with a peppery leaf salad and serve the rest of the gooseberry jam in a bowl on the side.

Salmon & sea trout

Salmon is one of our most popular fish. I am a big fan of wild salmon, obviously, but I'm also impressed by the quality of organic farmed salmon. Eating farmed salmon is undoubtedly a positive step, as it takes the pressure off wild salmon, which in time, should allow stocks to return to a safe level for sustainable fishing. Wild salmon have to be the most amazing survivors in the fish world. They spawn at the heads of rivers, then travel downstream and out to sea when they are 2 or 3 years old to feed on protein-rich sand eels, sprats and prawns. After a few years, when they are strong and big enough for the journey back, they return to their birthplace to breed. So salmon are anadramous, which basically means they can live in both fresh water and salt water, but not easily. Only the strongest survive the change to salt water – just one in every one hundred fish. Wild salmon truly demand respect. On top of an extraordinarily demanding life cycle, they must avoid being caught on rod and line, or by an otter, pike, heron or cormorant. And once out to sea they are targeted by seals, dolphins and sharks, not to mention air attacks from gulls and eagles. Truly amazing!

Sea trout looks like salmon, but it is a distant cousin and originates from the same egg as the brown trout. Quite why some trout are born sea trout and others brown trout is a bit of a mystery but it is thought to have a lot to do with the amount of food available and the place they are born. Like salmon, the sea trout embarks on the journey to the sea, but remains inshore until it has reached a good size and has a bigger survival rate as a consequence. It also returns upstream to breed – with the brown trout – much sooner. As for eating quality, sea trout is up there with salmon and the same cooking processes can be applied to both fish. I'm a big fan of lightly curing sea trout, then giving it a light hot smoke before making a simple beetroot salad to serve it with.

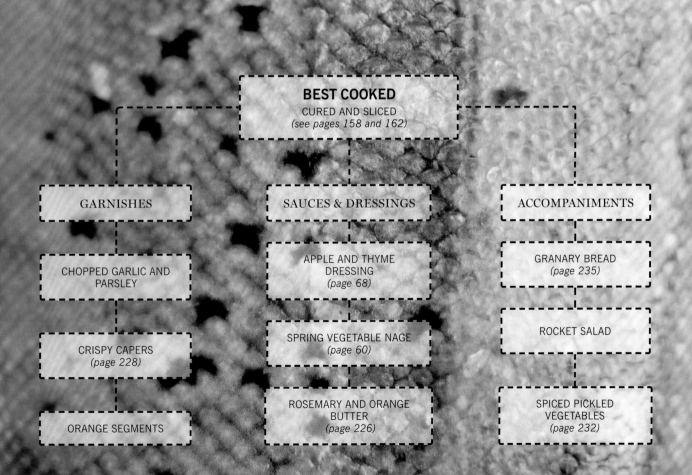

BEST COOKED
CURED AND SLICED
(see pages 158 and 162)

GARNISHES

SAUCES & DRESSINGS

ACCOMPANIMENTS

CHOPPED GARLIC AND PARSLEY

APPLE AND THYME DRESSING
(page 68)

GRANARY BREAD
(page 235)

CRISPY CAPERS
(page 228)

SPRING VEGETABLE NAGE
(page 60)

ROCKET SALAD

ORANGE SEGMENTS

ROSEMARY AND ORANGE BUTTER
(page 226)

SPICED PICKLED VEGETABLES
(page 232)

Cured salmon with beetroot dressing and horseradish cream

This has been on my Seafood and Grill menu since day one, thanks to the wizardry of head chef Pete Biggs. Horseradish, beetroot and salmon work so well together. You'll need to start well ahead as the salmon needs to be cured for around 30 hours. Slice your salmon a little thicker than the usual smoked salmon to get the full flavour and lovely texture.

Serves 10

1 side of organic farmed or wild salmon

Cornish sea salt and freshly ground black pepper

Cure

1kg beetroot, peeled and cut into 3cm cubes

1 tsp fennel seeds

small bunch of tarragon, leaves only

500g caster sugar

1kg sea salt

Beetroot dressing

1kg raw beetroot, washed

50ml white wine vinegar

2 banana shallots, peeled and finely chopped

2 garlic cloves, peeled and finely chopped

about 200ml olive oil

2 tsp chopped chives

Horseradish cream

500ml double cream

3 tbsp good-quality creamed horseradish, or to taste

To serve

500g watercress, trimmed and washed

½ quantity treacle bread (page 235)

Check the salmon for any pin bones and trim as necessary. For the cure, put the beetroot, fennel seeds, tarragon, sugar and sea salt in a food processor and blitz until smooth. Lay the salmon on a tray (that will hold the salmon and cure) and spoon the cure over the salmon. Cover with cling film and leave to cure in the fridge for 10 hours.

Turn the side of salmon over and spoon over the cure. Re-cover and return to the fridge for another 20 hours.

Wash off the cure and pat the salmon dry. At this stage your cured salmon is ready to eat.

For the beetroot dressing, place the unpeeled beetroot in a saucepan, cover with water and add a pinch of salt and a dash of the wine vinegar. Bring to a simmer and cook for about 20 minutes until the beetroot is tender, but not soft. Leave to cool in the water and then drain and peel. Cut the beetroot into 5mm dice and place in a bowl with the shallots, garlic, some salt and pepper, and the rest of the wine vinegar. Cover with the olive oil and set aside. When ready to serve, stir in the chives.

For the horseradish cream, whisk the cream until softly peaking, then fold in the horseradish. Taste and add a little seasoning, or a little more horseradish if you like. Spoon into a small serving dish.

To serve, slice the salmon across the grain and lay the slices overlapping on individual plates. Put a dollop of horseradish cream next to the fish. Scatter over the diced beetroot and add a spoonful of the dressing that has formed in the dish. Finish with watercress leaves and serve with slices of treacle bread.

Charcoal salmon with roast garlic, lemon and parsley pearl barley

This dish came about one day when I had some broken charcoal wafers in one hand and salmon belly trimmings in the other, which some claim to be the tastiest part of the fish. I don't like wastage so I cured the salmon trimmings, coated them with the broken biscuits and deep-fried them. Paired with the flavours of garlic, lemon and parsley, the result was amazing.

Serves 4

4 salmon fillets, about 100g each

100g salt

100g caster sugar

finely grated zest of 1 lemon

100g charcoal wafer cheese biscuits

100g plain flour

1 egg, beaten

oil for deep-frying

Roast garlic, lemon and parsley pearl barley

1 garlic bulb

olive oil for cooking

50g unsalted butter

2 shallots, peeled and chopped

150g pearl barley

100ml dry white wine

500ml roast fish or vegetable stock (page 222)

75g Parmesan, grated

75g mascarpone

4 tbsp finely chopped parsley

½ lemon, in peeled segments

Cornish sea salt and freshly ground black pepper

To finish

mustard cress to garnish

olive oil to drizzle

8 unpeeled garlic cloves for roasting (optional)

Heat the oven to 200°C/Gas 6. Check the salmon for any pin bones.

For the pearl barley, halve the garlic bulb widthways and place on a piece of foil. Sprinkle with salt and drizzle with olive oil. Seal the foil and place on a baking tray with the garlic cloves for the garnish if using. Roast for 45 minutes (20 minutes for the individual cloves), then set aside.

Meanwhile, lay the salmon on a tray. Mix the salt, sugar and lemon zest together and sprinkle over the salmon. Cover with cling film and refrigerate for 30 minutes.

To cook the barley, heat a large saucepan over a medium heat and add the butter and a drizzle of olive oil. When bubbling, add the shallots and cook, without colouring, for 1 minute. Add the pearl barley to the pan and cook for 1 minute, stirring all the time. Next add the white wine and simmer until reduced right down, almost to nothing. Now add the stock and simmer until the barley is tender, but retains a slight bite. Set aside to cool.

Wash the cure off the salmon and cut into slices, about 1cm thick. Blitz the charcoal wafers in a food processor until finely ground. Put the flour, beaten egg and charcoal crumbs into 3 separate bowls. Pass the salmon through the flour and pat off the excess, then dip into the beaten egg and finally pass through the charcoal wafer crumbs to coat. Set aside on a plate.

When ready to serve, heat the oil in a deep-fryer or other suitable deep, heavy pan to 180°C. Deep-fry the salmon in the hot oil, in batches if necessary, for 2 minutes until crispy. Remove and drain on kitchen paper, then sprinkle with salt; keep warm while cooking the rest.

Meanwhile, return the pan of barley to a medium-low heat and warm through for 1 minute. Peel the roasted garlic bulb and stir through the barley with the Parmesan, mascarpone and parsley. Take off the heat, add the lemon segments and season with salt and pepper to taste.

Spoon the barley onto 4 warmed plates and top with the salmon. Finish with mustard cress, a trickle of olive oil and the roasted garlic cloves, if using.

Citrus marinated sea trout with samphire and crispy oysters

This is a way of pickling fish that is good on the day it's prepared, but even better the following day. Ingredients from the estuary rather than the sea inspire this dish, the contrasting textures of the soft sea trout and crunchy samphire leaves working perfectly with the crispy, ozone-fresh oyster.

Serves 4 as a starter

1 large or 2 medium sea trout fillets, about 300g in total, filleted, trimmed and pin-boned

4 tsp coriander seeds

4 tsp fennel seeds

2 tsp black peppercorns

3 tsp salt

3 tsp sugar

finely grated zest and juice of 2 lemons

finely grated zest and juice of 2 limes

finely grated zest and juice of 1 orange

light rapeseed oil for cooking

2 shallots, peeled and cut into rings

2 garlic cloves, peeled, green germ removed and chopped

100ml dry white wine

200g samphire, trimmed and washed

knob of butter

100ml olive oil

Crispy oysters

4 Pacific oysters, shucked, juices retained (see page 258)

50g plain flour

1 egg, beaten

75g Japanese panko breadcrumbs

oil for deep-frying

In a dry frying pan over a medium heat, toast the coriander seeds, fennel seeds and peppercorns until they start to pop. Transfer to a spice grinder, add the salt and sugar, and grind until fine.

Lay the sea trout fillet, skin side down in a deep tray, sprinkle with the spice mix and rub it in carefully. Heat a large non-stick frying pan and add a good drizzle of oil. When the oil is hot, lay the sea trout skin side down in the pan (cutting it in half to fit in the pan if necessary) and cook for 1 minute or until golden. Carefully lift out the sea trout and place back on the tray. Scatter the citrus zests over the fish.

Put the frying pan back over a medium heat and add a little oil. Add the shallot rings and garlic and cook for 1 minute. Pour in the white wine and citrus juices and simmer for 3 minutes. Pour the marinade over the trout, making sure it is covered, and then lay some cling film over the top to keep everything submerged. Chill for at least 5 hours, preferably overnight.

For the crispy oysters, pat the oysters dry on kitchen paper. Have the flour, egg and breadcrumbs ready in 3 separate bowls. One by one, pass the oysters through the flour, egg and breadcrumbs and place on a plate. Set aside until serving.

Blanch the samphire in boiling water for 1 minute, then drain and briefly glaze in a covered pan with a knob of butter, adding the shallots from the marinade and tossing to combine.

When ready to serve, heat your oven to 120°C/Gas ½. Take the trout from the fridge and place in the oven for 10 minutes, just to take off the chill. For the dressing, strain off 100ml of the marinade into a bowl, add the 100ml olive oil and saved oyster juices and whisk to emulsify. Pour into a jug.

Meanwhile, heat the oil in a deep-fryer or other deep, heavy pan to 180°C. Add the oysters and deep-fry for 1 minute, then drain on kitchen paper.

To serve, place the sea trout fillet and samphire on a warm serving platter. Spoon over the dressing and top with the crispy oysters. Serve at once.

I love good quality smoked fish and whenever possible I like to smoke the fish myself. Gone are the days of nasty pre-packed smoked kippers – unnaturally yellow in colour with that strange star-shaped butter pat on top. Now, even if home-smoking isn't an option, you can buy good-quality smoked fish. Obviously, the calibre of a smoked fish is largely determined by the freshness and quality of the original catch, but the curing process plays a major role as well. Back in the old days, smoking was a way of preserving your catch and making it go further through the year. Now smoked fish is enjoyed purely for its special flavour, but there is a lot of work involved in getting a top-quality product and that brings a higher price tag.

Smoked fish

If possible, source your smoked fish from the excellent artisan smokeries dotted around our coastline. Or consider investing in your own hot or cold smoker and experiment with different cures and woods for smoking. Expect a degree of trial and error to begin with, but in time you'll find you can successfully smoke pretty much anything you buy or catch yourself.

So what is the difference between hot and cold smoked fish? With cold smoking the temperature barely touches 25°C. The curing process smokes and dries the fish, imparting flavour, but the fish remains raw. Before cold smoking, fish is always salted or brined, both to improve the texture and preserve it. Hot smoking does cook the fish and could be described as roasting with the addition of smoky aromas. The pre-salting or brining is much less, as the intention is to eat the fish straight away, unlike cold smoked fish which keeps for longer. Hot smoking is more suited to oily fish as white fish are inclined to dry out with the higher temperature.

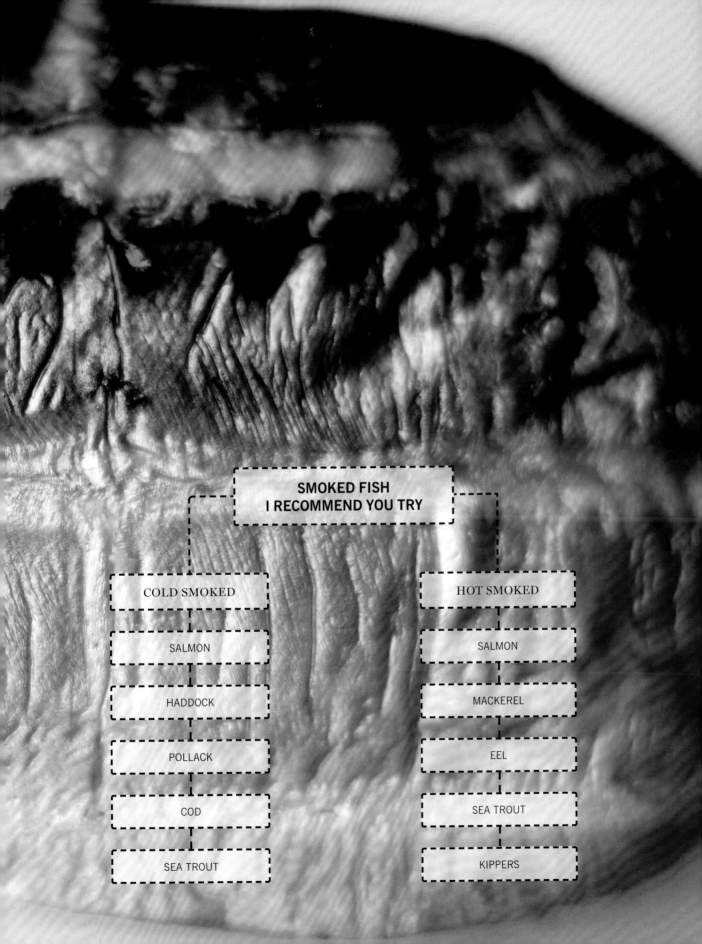

**SMOKED FISH
I RECOMMEND YOU TRY**

COLD SMOKED

SALMON

HADDOCK

POLLACK

COD

SEA TROUT

HOT SMOKED

SALMON

MACKEREL

EEL

SEA TROUT

KIPPERS

Smoked haddock with mustard sauce and sea spinach

There is something very comforting about smoked haddock and this is the sort of dish I enjoy on a Sunday evening. I use locally foraged sea spinach here, but ordinary spinach or watercress would be fine if sea vegetables are not an option. The grainy mustard balances the smokiness of the fish perfectly.

Serves 4

4 smoked haddock fillets, 200g each, skinned

olive oil for cooking

4 garlic cloves (unpeeled)

handful of thyme sprigs

1 shallot, peeled and finely chopped

100ml cider

2 tbsp cider vinegar

30ml double cream

100g unsalted butter, diced

2 tsp wholegrain mustard

500g sea spinach, washed and trimmed

Cornish sea salt and freshly ground black pepper

Preheat the oven to 200°C/Gas 6. Place each smoked haddock fillet on a sheet of foil (large enough to enclose the fish). Drizzle a little olive oil over the fish and add the garlic, thyme and a good grinding of pepper. Bring the extra foil up over the fish and fold the edges together to seal and form a parcel. Lay the parcels on a large baking tray and place in the oven to cook for 10 minutes.

Meanwhile, put the shallot, cider and cider vinegar into a saucepan and bring to a simmer. Let bubble until the liquid has reduced right down, almost to nothing, then add the cream. Now, over a very low heat, or moving the pan on and off the heat, whisk in the butter a piece at a time. When it is all incorporated, stir in the mustard and taste for seasoning, adding salt and pepper as required. Keep warm.

When the fish is almost ready, heat a saucepan over a medium heat and add a drizzle of olive oil. When hot, add the sea spinach and cook for 1 minute until wilted.

Open up the fish parcels. Pour any juices from the parcels into the spinach to season it, toss to mix and then drain.

Serve the smoked haddock fillets on warmed plates with the spinach alongside and the sauce in a bowl on the side.

Smoked mackerel and beetroot salad with horseradish mayonnaise

This is one of my favourite combinations of flavours – smoked mackerel and earthy beetroot with a touch of zingy hot horseradish and salty capers... I could enjoy it all day long. I like to serve this on a platter in the middle of the table for all to share. It works well with smoked salmon too.

Serves 4

8 smoked mackerel fillets, skinned

300g raw beetroot, peeled

olive oil for cooking and to dress

2 shallots, peeled and finely sliced

50ml red wine vinegar

3 tsp chopped dill

Cornish sea salt and freshly ground black pepper

Horseradish mayonnaise

2 egg yolks

juice of ½ lemon

2 tbsp horseradish cream

200ml light olive oil

To serve

mustard cress

crispy capers (page 228)

extra horseradish cream (if you can handle it!)

Check the smoked mackerel fillets for pin bones and break into large flakes. Slice the beetroot very thinly, using a mandolin if you have one.

Heat a non-stick pan over a medium heat and add a drizzle of olive oil. When hot, add the shallots and cook for 2 minutes until translucent. Season with salt and pepper and add the wine vinegar. Transfer to a plate to cool.

Put the sliced beetroot, shallots, chopped dill and a good drizzle of olive oil into a bowl and season with salt and pepper. Give it a good mix with your hands and leave to stand for at least 30 minutes.

For the horseradish mayonnaise, put the egg yolks, lemon juice and horseradish cream into a bowl and whisk together for 1 minute to combine. Slowly add the olive oil, drop by drop to begin with, then in a steady stream, whisking constantly, until the mixture is emulsified and thick. Season with salt and pepper to taste and reserve in the fridge.

Arrange the beetroot on a large platter and scatter the pieces of smoked mackerel on top. Dot the mayonnaise randomly all over the platter, using a piping bag fitted with a small plain nozzle for a neat presentation if you wish.

Scatter the mustard cress and crispy capers over the mackerel and serve, with extra horseradish mayonnaise on the side if you like.

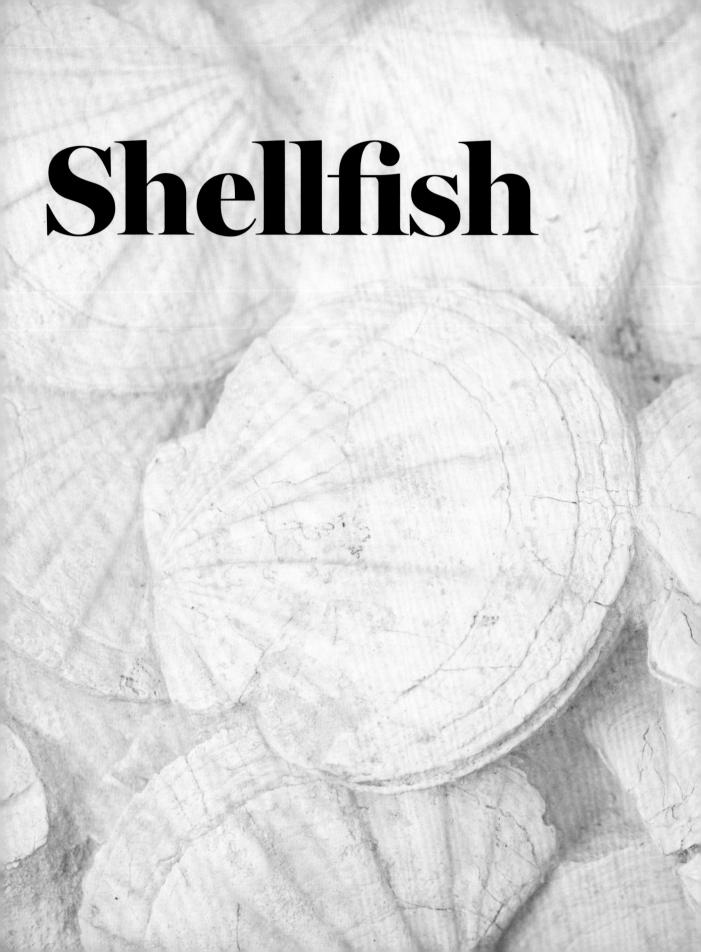

Shellfish

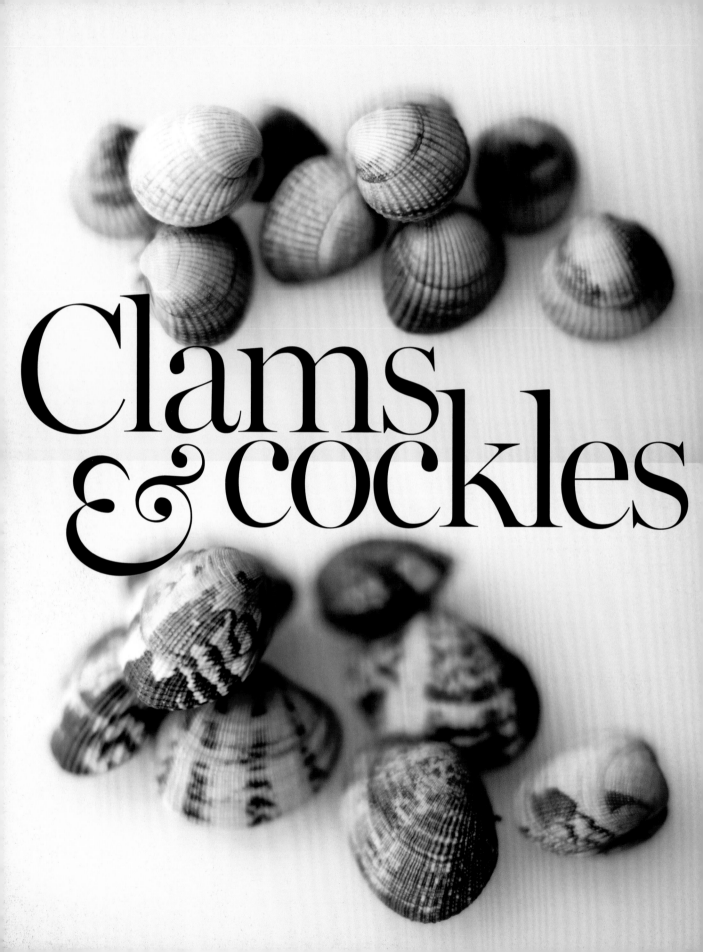

Clams
& cockles

Tasty, succulent clams can be found all around our coastline. Manila, surf and razor clams – all of which taste fantastic – are the most common varieties, but you might also come across carpet shells, sand gapers, hard shells, warty venus and other varieties at the right time of year. Local knowledge is the key. Some varieties are native; others have arrived on our shores and settled. With the exception of razor clams, which need to be treated slightly differently owing to their very different shape, clams can be cooked in the same way as mussels and cockles. Clams live in sandy, muddy and pebbly areas and you sometimes get the odd one that retains a bit of grit after washing. Accept this and don't let that ruin your enjoyment of these beauties. The best time to eat clams is from September to February, but don't worry about the sustainable aspect – there are loads of them!

My first taste of cockles was on Hastings seafront. My Grandad bought them from a fish and chip shop and, of course, we had them with malt vinegar… Since then I've used them in many different ways. Cockles are available all year, but I suggest you avoid them in the summer when they are spawning. They are common around the UK and are very sustainable. They are quite easy to gather yourself, but do ask around before you venture out with a rake and a bucket. Cockles live happily anywhere, including undesirable areas, so ask locals if the quality of the water is good enough for cockling. When you get your cockles home, it's best to purge them in a mixture of salt and water overnight to get rid of all the sand and mud before cooking them. Make sure you throw away any that are open as they will be dead. Mature cockles for eating are generally 2–3 years old; occasionally they live to 5 years but these are a little tough to eat.

BEST COOKED
STEAMED
(see page 178)

GARNISHES

CHOPPED PARSLEY AND GARLIC

CHOPPED GHERKINS

SLICED CHILLIES

SAUCES & DRESSINGS

CURRY SAUCE
(page 182)

BEER SAUCE
(cook clams or cockles in 150ml beer; use as a sauce)

ROSEMARY AND ORANGE BUTTER
(page 226)

ACCOMPANIMENTS

GRANARY BREAD
(page 235)

RED PEPPER MARMALADE
(page 152)

LINGUINE

Cider and leek soup with clams, cockles and quail's eggs

This is a fantastic warming soup when there is a chill in the air. I usually make a big cauldron of it, adding as many different shellfish as I can get my hands on, and let everyone tuck in and help themselves. The deep-fried quail's eggs aren't essential but they do give the soup a special finishing touch.

Serves 4

500g live clams, cleaned (as for mussels, see page 180)

500g live cockles, cleaned (see page 173)

light rapeseed oil for cooking

50g unsalted butter

3 shallots, peeled and chopped

4 leeks (white part only), washed and sliced

200g potatoes, peeled and finely sliced

1 litre fish stock

500ml cider

100ml double cream

Cornish sea salt and freshly ground black pepper

Deep-fried quail's eggs

12 quail's eggs

50g plain flour

1 egg, beaten

75g Japanese panko breadcrumbs

oil for deep-frying

Lemon, parsley and apple dressing

1 apple, peeled and cut into 5mm dice

1 tsp chopped parsley

75ml lemon oil (page 227)

To finish

shredded flat-leaf parsley

Place a large saucepan over a medium heat and when hot add a generous drizzle of oil and the butter. When the butter is bubbling, add the shallots and leeks with a pinch of salt and cook for 2 minutes until they are turning translucent. Now add the potatoes and cook, stirring, for 1 minute.

Add the fish stock and half of the cider and simmer until the potatoes are soft. Add the cream and bring to the boil. Transfer the soup to a blender and blitz until smooth. Return to a clean pan and set aside.

Place a large saucepan (that has a tight-fitting lid) over a medium heat. When hot, add the clams, cockles and remaining cider and put the lid on. Cook for 3 minutes until the shells have opened, then drain in a colander over a bowl to catch the liquor. When cool enough to handle, pick the meat from the shells, keeping a few clams and cockles in their shell for serving. Place in a bowl and keep cool, with the reserved liquor, until ready to serve.

For the quail's eggs, bring a pan of water to a simmer, then carefully lower the eggs into it and simmer for 2 minutes. Remove to a bowl of iced water and leave to cool for 5 minutes, then drain and peel the eggs. Put the flour, beaten egg and breadcrumbs into 3 separate bowls. Dry the eggs thoroughly and pass them first through the flour, then the egg and finally coat in the breadcrumbs. Set aside until ready to serve.

For the lemon, parsley and apple dressing, combine the apple, chopped parsley and lemon oil in a bowl and season with salt and pepper to taste.

To serve, heat the oil in a deep-fryer or other suitable deep, heavy pan to 180°C. Deep-fry the coated quail's eggs for 1 minute until golden and crispy. Bring the soup to a simmer and add some of the reserved shellfish poaching liquid, to adjust the taste and the consistency to your liking. Drain the deep-fried quail's eggs on kitchen paper and season with a little salt.

Add the picked shellfish to the soup and share equally between 4 warmed bowls, or serve in a tureen. Finish the soup with the reserved clams and cockles in shells, the quail's eggs, dressing and a sprinkling of parsley.

Grilled razor clams with savoury crumb topping and Pernod cream

Razor clams are very tasty and I've been a big fan for a long time. In this dish the flavours of fennel, Pernod and razor clams dance together beautifully. When the heat of the grill hits the clams they pop open, releasing their tasty juice, which forms the base for an amazing sauce. Make sure your razor clams are alive!

Serves 4

20 live razor clams, well rinsed

75g fine breadcrumbs

1 shallot, peeled and finely chopped

1 garlic clove, peeled and finely chopped

2 tbsp wild fennel herb (if unavailable use dill or fennel tops)

finely pared zest of 1 lemon, finely chopped

50g Parmesan, grated

50ml olive oil, plus extra to drizzle

75ml Pernod

100ml double cream

50g unsalted butter, in pieces

Cornish sea salt and freshly ground black pepper

Preheat your grill to its highest setting. In a large bowl, mix the breadcrumbs, shallot, garlic, fennel herb, lemon zest and Parmesan together well. Season with salt and pepper and add the olive oil to bind the mixture. Set aside.

Lay the clams on a large baking tray, season with salt and drizzle over some olive oil and the Pernod. Place the clams under the grill until they pop open; this will take about 3 minutes. As they open, pull them out from under the grill and carefully remove the meat from the shell. Strain the juice released by the clams into a pan and let bubble over a medium heat to reduce to about 100ml.

Prepare the clams, removing the dark part (see page 259), then roughly chop them and mix through the crumbs. Spoon the mixture back into the shells, dividing it equally. Set aside while you finish the sauce. (Rather than chop them, you can simply cover the whole clams with the crumb mixture if you prefer.)

Stir the cream into the clam juice and simmer for 2 minutes. Taste for seasoning and then whisk in the butter.

To serve, place the clams back under the grill for 3–4 minutes until golden. Divide between warmed plates and spoon some sauce over each clam. Serve at once.

Cockle and clam kedgeree

The first time I tasted kedgeree was at Billingsgate fish market in London. Peter Kromberg, the head chef where I was working, regularly took the young chefs to the market and we ended our visit with a breakfast of kedgeree. I've loved it ever since. My version has some smoked fish, like the traditional one, but I like to include cockles and clams as well.

Serves 4

200g smoked haddock fillet

200g live cockles, cleaned (see page 173)

200g live clams, cleaned (as for mussels, see page 180)

700ml roast fish stock (page 222)

light rapeseed oil for cooking

50g unsalted butter

2 shallots, peeled and finely chopped

1 leek (white part only), washed and finely sliced

1 celery stick, finely sliced

1 garlic clove, peeled and chopped

300g long-grain or basmati rice, washed and drained

pinch of saffron strands

½ tsp mild curry powder

3 medium eggs

2 tsp chopped coriander leaves, plus a few leaves to finish

lemon wedges to serve

Preheat the oven to 200°C/Gas 6. Remove the skin from the smoked haddock and cut the fillet into 2cm dice; set aside.

Place a large saucepan (that has a tight-fitting lid) over a high heat. When the pan is really hot, add the cockles and clams with 100ml of the fish stock and put the lid on. Steam for 2 minutes until the shells open. Tip the contents of the pan into a colander over a bowl to catch the liquor.

When the shellfish are cool enough to handle, pick out the meat from the shells, leaving some in their shells for serving. Place in a bowl and keep cool until ready to serve. Strain the liquor though a fine sieve or muslin to remove any grit or sand; reserve.

To cook the rice, place an ovenproof pan (that has a lid) over a medium heat. When it is hot, add a drizzle of oil and the butter. When the butter is bubbling, add the shallots, leek, celery and garlic and cook, stirring, for 2 minutes, to soften without colouring. Add the rice and cook, stirring, for 1 minute. Add the saffron, curry powder, remaining fish stock and the reserved shellfish juice. Bring to a simmer and cover with a lid. Place the pan in the oven and cook for 15 minutes until tender.

Meanwhile, add the eggs to a pan of simmering water, return to a simmer and cook for 6 minutes. Drain and briefly run under cold water, then peel. Quarter the eggs lengthways.

When the rice is ready, remove the pan from the oven and add the smoked haddock, clams, cockles, chopped coriander and egg quarters. Gently fold the ingredients through the rice and season with salt and pepper to taste. The heat of the rice will gently cook the smoked haddock pieces. Scatter over a few coriander leaves.

Serve the kedgeree straight from the pan into warmed bowls, with lemon wedges, and bread and butter on the side if you like.

Mussels

I am fortunate to have an abundance of fantastic mussels growing on the Camel Estuary, a stone's throw from the restaurant in Porthilly Bay. Nurtured by father and son Tim and Luke Marshall, mussels grow happily on the estuary farm, as long as they manage to avoid the ever-hungry shore crabs and various sea birds. Farmed mussels are safest to eat, as they are held in clean seawater and treated with ultraviolet light for 48 hours to get rid of nasty bacteria before they are sold. It is rare to find wild mussels in the shops nowadays. The common wild mussel has a lot to contend with as it clings to rocks, seaweed and other mussels. Constantly threatened by predators, it also has to survive extremes of temperature and a fair amount of battering when conditions get tough. You can gather wild mussels yourself at the beach, provided you take some precautions to avoid ghastly food poisoning. Mussels can filter up to 1 litre of seawater per hour, but that water needs to be clean. Try to stick to beach and rocky areas with fast running tides, well away from any sewage outlets and harbours. Also avoid collecting mussels in hotter months, when bacteria will grow at a faster rate.

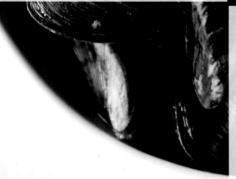

Mussels are an excellent, sustainable seafood and easy to prepare. Before cooking, check that they are in good condition and closed. Tap any open mussels sharply – they will close up if they're alive, otherwise discard them. Similarly throw away any mussels that have cracked or damaged shells. Pull away the hairy 'beard', attached to one end of the mussel. Farmed mussels should only need a quick rinse to clean them without washing away flavour, but if mussels are sandy or dirty you'll need to give them a more thorough wash or a quick soak in cold water.

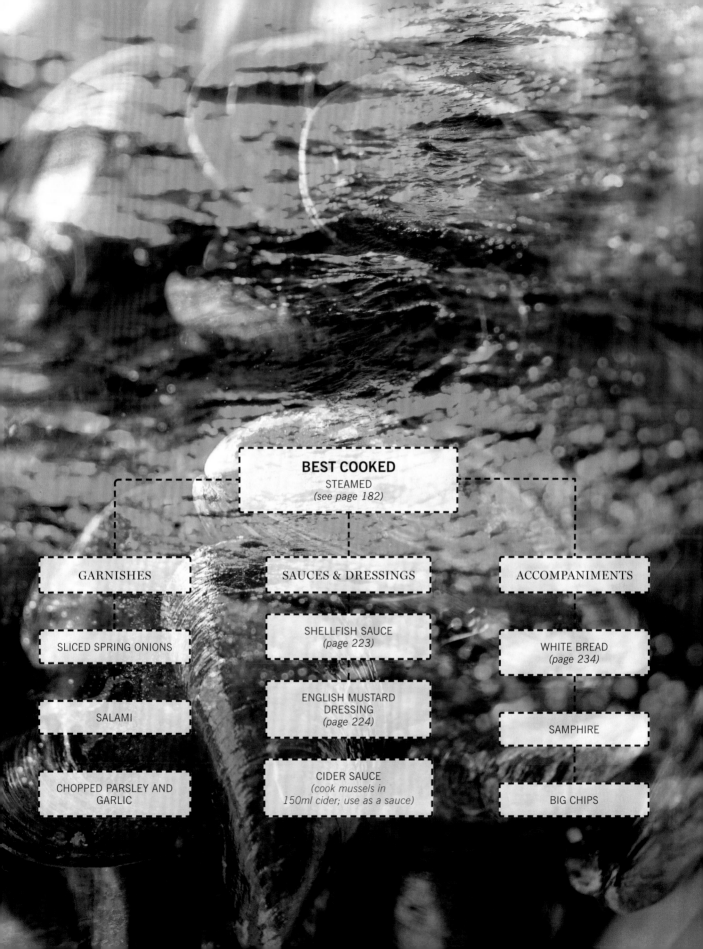

BEST COOKED
STEAMED
(see page 182)

GARNISHES

SAUCES & DRESSINGS

ACCOMPANIMENTS

SLICED SPRING ONIONS

SHELLFISH SAUCE
(page 223)

WHITE BREAD
(page 234)

SALAMI

ENGLISH MUSTARD
DRESSING
(page 224)

SAMPHIRE

CHOPPED PARSLEY AND
GARLIC

CIDER SAUCE
*(cook mussels in
150ml cider; use as a sauce)*

BIG CHIPS

Mussel, spinach and cauliflower curry with crispy mussels

My staff enjoy a good curry and this curry sauce, based on a recipe I picked up from a Goan chef, is the one I always make when it's my turn to cook 'staff tea'. Caramelising the onions and cooking out the curry paste gives the curry a unique taste.

Serves 4

1kg live mussels, cleaned (see page 180)

1 cauliflower, divided into florets

100g spinach, trimmed and washed

50g plain flour for coating

oil for deep-frying

2 tbsp chopped coriander leaves

Cornish sea salt and freshly ground black pepper

Curry sauce

2 garlic cloves, peeled and chopped

50g fresh root ginger, peeled and chopped

1 tsp ground turmeric

1 tsp ground cumin

20g tamarind paste

3 red chillies

1 tsp mild curry powder

light rapeseed oil for cooking

2 onions, peeled and sliced

4 tomatoes, chopped

500ml water

400ml tin coconut milk

Batter coating

50g plain flour

50g cornflour

about 200ml soda water

First make the curry sauce. Put the garlic, ginger, turmeric, cumin, tamarind paste, chillies and curry powder into a food processor and blend to a paste. Heat a large saucepan over a medium heat and add a drizzle of oil. When hot, add the onions and sweat for at least 5 minutes until well coloured and caramelised. Transfer to a plate. Clean the pan, place it back on a low heat and add a drizzle of oil. When hot, add the curry paste and sweat gently for 4 minutes, making sure it doesn't catch on the pan. Add the caramelised onions along with the tomatoes and cook for 3 minutes. Next add the water and coconut milk and leave the sauce to cook for 1 hour on a low heat.

Meanwhile, place another pan (that has a tight-fitting lid) over a medium heat. When hot, add 20 mussels with a splash of water and put the lid on. Steam for 2 minutes or until opened and then remove them from the pan; discard any unopened mussels. Leave until cool enough to handle, then shell the mussels. Place in a bowl, cover and refrigerate until ready to serve.

For the batter, mix the flour and cornflour together in a bowl and season with salt and pepper. Stir in enough soda water to give a smooth batter consistency. Chill until needed.

Season the curry sauce with salt and pepper to taste. If it is too thick, add a little more water. Add the cauliflower to the sauce and cook for 5 minutes. Now add the remaining mussels in shells along with the spinach. Cover tightly and cook for 4 minutes until the mussels open; discard any that remain closed.

While the curry is cooking, heat the oil for deep-frying in a deep-fryer or deep, heavy pan to 180°C. Pass the chilled shelled mussels through the flour to coat, patting off the excess. You'll need to deep-fry them in 2 batches. One by one, dip them into the batter to coat and lower into the hot oil. Deep-fry for a minute or so until crispy. Remove and drain on kitchen paper and season them with a little salt.

Add the chopped coriander to the curry and divide between 4 warmed bowls. Top each serving with 5 crispy mussels and serve at once.

Mussel and saffron quiche with fennel and rocket salad

This is a lovely way of cooking mussels when you have a bit more time on your hands. The saffron lends a subtle flavour and the fennel and rocket salad provides a crisp, fresh contrast. This recipe also works well with smoked fish in place of the mussels; use 300g filleted smoked haddock or mackerel.

Serves 6

Pastry

250g plain flour

150g unsalted butter, diced

1 tsp fine sea salt

1 egg, beaten

1 tbsp cold milk

eggwash (1 egg yolk, beaten with 2 tsp milk)

Filling

1kg live mussels, cleaned (see page 180)

6 eggs

600ml double cream

250g mature Cheddar (ideally Davidstow Crackler), diced

2 bunches of spring onions, trimmed and sliced

pinch of saffron strands

2 tbsp chopped parsley

2 tbsp chopped dill

Cornish sea salt and freshly ground black pepper

Fennel and rocket salad

1 fennel bulb, trimmed

2 handfuls of rocket leaves, washed

juice of ½ lemon, plus lemon wedges to serve

50ml olive oil

To make the pastry, put the flour, butter and salt into a food processor and process until the mixture resembles fine breadcrumbs. Add the egg and milk and pulse briefly until the dough comes together. Shape the pastry into a disc, wrap in cling film and rest in the fridge for 1 hour.

Place a large pan (that has a tight-fitting lid) over a medium heat. When hot, add the mussels with a splash of water and put the lid on. Steam for 2 minutes or until opened and then remove them from the pan; discard any unopened mussels. Leave until cool enough to handle, then pick the mussels out of their shells (you should have about 300g). Place in a bowl, cover and refrigerate until needed.

Preheat the oven to 220°C/Gas 7. Roll out the pastry on a floured surface to the thickness of a £1 coin and use to line six 10cm, 2cm deep, loose-based individual flan tins. Line the pastry cases with a disc of greaseproof paper and add a layer of baking beans. Chill for 10 minutes. Bake the pastry cases for 15 minutes, then remove the paper and baking beans and brush the inside of the pastry with eggwash. Turn the oven down to 160°C/Gas 3.

For the filling, lightly beat the eggs and cream together in a bowl and season with salt and pepper. Scatter the cheese, spring onions, mussels, saffron, parsley and dill evenly into the tart cases and pour over the egg mixture. Bake for 20 minutes, until the custard is set and the pastry is golden brown. Leave to cool slightly.

For the fennel and rocket salad, finely slice the fennel, using a mandolin if you have one. Place in a salad bowl with the rocket leaves and dress with the lemon juice and olive oil.

Serve the tarts warm or at room temperature, with the fennel and rocket salad and lemon wedges.

Oysters

I serve two types of oyster at my restaurants: farmed Pacific and wild native. To me, the wild native oyster is a treasure to be respected… and never, ever cooked! To fully enjoy a wild native, open it up and eat it – it's as simple as that. I feel differently about farmed oysters. Yes, I love to eat them live, but I also think they have a special quality when cooked. Their texture changes on cooking and they still taste wonderful.

The wild native oyster lives in estuaries and shallow water, hiding in muddy or sandy beds. All oysters draw in seawater and filter up to 6 litres a day, taking the oxygen and nutrients they need to live and grow, so it goes without saying that water quality is a vital consideration when gathering wild oysters. A hundred years ago, native oysters were abundant, cheap and eaten by all – rich and poor. Nowadays, partly because of the effects of pollution, natives are much rarer and considered a luxury food. As they are a protected species they can only be harvested outside of their spawning season, which is from May to the end of August. I buy my native oysters from a fisherman who collects them in the old-fashioned way from the Helford River in Cornwall, which helps to keep the fishing sustainable. In many parts of the country the native oyster is listed as a threatened species, so if you happen to find one, double check before helping yourself, as you could be breaking the law.

When buying oysters it is very important that you know where they are from and that they are tightly closed. Never eat an oyster that is open; it will be dead. You might be in for a treat if you happen to be on a beach near an oyster farm, as Pacific oysters have been breaking loose for years and growing happily (and quite quickly) in wild waters. If you plan on eating them, just check that they are nowhere near a sewage outlet or harbour. If you're confident, then eat away.

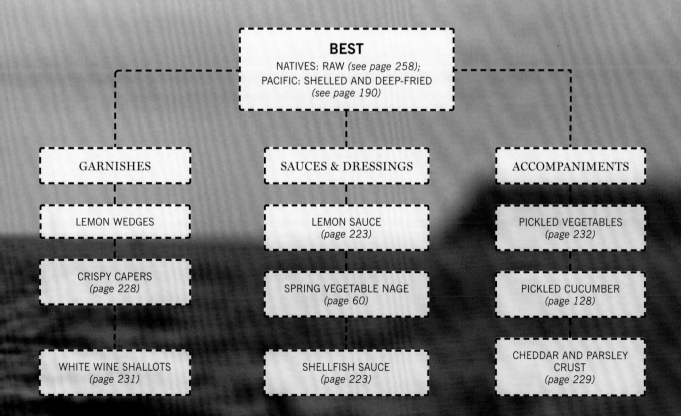

BEST
NATIVES: RAW *(see page 258)*;
PACIFIC: SHELLED AND DEEP-FRIED
(see page 190)

GARNISHES

LEMON WEDGES

CRISPY CAPERS
(page 228)

WHITE WINE SHALLOTS
(page 231)

SAUCES & DRESSINGS

LEMON SAUCE
(page 223)

SPRING VEGETABLE NAGE
(page 60)

SHELLFISH SAUCE
(page 223)

ACCOMPANIMENTS

PICKLED VEGETABLES
(page 232)

PICKLED CUCUMBER
(page 128)

CHEDDAR AND PARSLEY
CRUST
(page 229)

Watercress soup with Porthilly oysters and smoked oil

Watercress and oysters work so well together and here smoked oil adds another amazing taste dimension. If you haven't time to prepare the oil, then use a good-quality olive oil or even my lemon oil (on page 227). You can also use rocket in place of watercress, or a mixture of spinach and watercress or rocket if you like.

Serves 4

8 oysters, shucked (see page 258), juices retained

light rapeseed oil for cooking

1 small onion, peeled and sliced

2 garlic cloves, peeled, green germ removed, and sliced

1 large potato, peeled and thinly sliced

about 1 litre vegetable stock (page 222)

2 large bunches of watercress, leaves only, washed

Cornish sea salt and freshly ground black pepper

smoked oil (page 227), to serve

Heat a medium saucepan and add a good drizzle of rapeseed oil. Add the onion and garlic and cook for 1 minute, without colouring. Add the sliced potato and then pour on enough of the vegetable stock to cover. Simmer for about 10 minutes until the potato is cooked. Transfer the contents of the pan to a blender.

Place a frying pan over a medium-high heat and add a little oil. Now add the watercress and fry briefly until just wilted. Add the watercress to the blender and blitz for 3 minutes or until smooth. Season with salt to taste. Unless serving straight away, chill the soup over ice to retain its vivid green colour.

When ready to serve, pour the watercress soup base into a pan, add the reserved oyster juices and enough of the remaining stock to give the required consistency. Taste and adjust the seasoning. Heat through gently.

Divide the soup between 4 warmed bowls. Add the oysters and finish each serving with a drizzle of smoked oil to serve.

Crispy oysters with pickled vegetables and oyster mayonnaise

My kids love this recipe. At the oyster festival in Rock last year, of the various different fish burgers we made, the crispy oyster and pickled veg burgers were by far our best seller. I was most impressed that many of our satisfied customers were kids trying oysters for the first time. You don't have to put the crispy oysters in bread rolls, but it's a great way to eat them.

Serves 4

12 oysters, shucked (see page 258), juices retained

50g plain flour for coating

1 egg, beaten

75g Japanese panko breadcrumbs or day-old white breadcrumbs

oil for deep-frying

Cornish sea salt and freshly ground black pepper

Oyster mayonnaise

2 egg yolks

juice of ½ lemon

2 oysters, shucked (see page 258), juices retained

300ml light rapeseed oil

To serve

4 white rolls (page 234), or use good-quality bought bread rolls (optional)

spiced pickled vegetables (page 232)

lemon wedges

First make the oyster mayonnaise. Put the egg yolks, lemon juice and oysters into a food processor and blend for 30 seconds. With the motor running, slowly add the oil until it's all incorporated and you have a thick mayonnaise. Add the reserved oyster juices (including those from the other 12 shucked oysters) and season with salt to taste. Cover and refrigerate until serving.

When you are ready to serve, put the flour, beaten egg and breadcrumbs into separate bowls and season the flour with salt and pepper. Heat the oil in a deep-fryer or other suitable deep, heavy pan to 180°C. One by one, pass the oysters through the flour, then the egg and finally the breadcrumbs to coat thoroughly, laying them out on a tray ready to cook.

Split and toast the bread rolls, if using, and spread with some oyster mayonnaise. If not serving rolls, rinse and dry the oyster shells.

Drain the pickled vegetables. Deep-fry the oysters in the hot oil for 1 minute until crispy, then remove and drain on kitchen paper.

Pile a generous amount of pickled vegetables on the bottom half of each roll, top with 3 deep-fried oysters and sandwich together with the top halves of the rolls. Alternatively, serve the pickled veg and crispy oysters in the cleaned oyster shells, adding a blob of mayonnaise to each one. Serve with lemon wedges and extra mayonnaise on the side.

Scallops

Like mussels and oysters, these bivalves are filter feeders, but unlike their relatives, scallops are pretty mobile, swimming and moving around the ocean at different times of the year. Whenever their rows of many eyes – arranged along the edge of their shells – sense danger on the horizon, they swim off at an impressive speed. A flock of scallops swimming through the sea is an amazing sight. Scallops can live well into double figures, but they are best harvested and eaten when 3–5 years old. You can tell the age of a scallop by the rings on its shell, each ring roughly representing a year. Dark-shelled scallops are from northern rocky coastlines, while pale-shelled scallops are from southern sandy locations. The best time to eat scallops is from December until late spring; make sure you avoid them during the summer, when they are spawning.

There are two types of scallops in the UK: the king and the queen. King scallops will grow up to 15cm across, while queens never reach more than 10cm. Scallop diving is the most sustainable way to catch these shellfish, far preferable to the commercial dragging method. Hauling a huge net attached to a beam over the seabed causes a lot of devastation, as it takes everything and breaks things in its path, so other species are often wiped out in the search for prized scallops. But scallop divers can adversely affect sustainability too, as they tend to pick out the larger scallops which are at their peak for reproduction and should really be left alone. It's important that everyone who is involved in scallop fishing is respectful. Scallops are wonderfully succulent and sweet. We should be able to enjoy them as a treat with a clear conscience.

BEST
EITHER RAW *(see page 194)*
OR PAN-FRIED *(page 196)*

GARNISHES	SAUCES & DRESSINGS	ACCOMPANIMENTS
RED WINE SHALLOTS *(page 231)*	SMOKED OIL *(page 227)*	PICKLED VEGETABLES *(page 232)*
LIME WEDGES	TOMATO KETCHUP *(page 233)*	ROASTED ROOT VEGETABLES *(page 20)*
CHOPPED PARSLEY AND GARLIC	ANCHOVY AND TARRAGON BUTTER *(page 226)*	PICKLED CHICORY *(page 22)*

Scallop tartare with pickled beetroot, bacon and apple

You need the freshest of amazing scallops for this dish. It's a lovely starter for a dinner party, though I also like to serve it as a lazy lunch. The pickled beetroot and apple work so well with the sweet fresh scallop and salty bacon.

Serves 4

300g scallops, cleaned and corals removed (see page 261)

4 rashers of smoked streaky bacon

1 apple

1 shallot, peeled and finely chopped

2 tsp chopped gherkin

2 tsp finely chopped chives

Cornish sea salt and freshly ground black pepper

Pickled beetroot

200g raw beetroot

2 tsp red wine vinegar

3 tsp sherry vinegar

1 shallot, peeled and finely chopped

1 garlic clove, peeled and finely chopped

1 tsp chopped thyme

4 tbsp olive oil

To assemble and serve

½ quantity mayonnaise (page 225)

4 slices of sourdough bread

handful of rocket leaves

lemon wedges

First prepare the pickled beetroot. Put the beetroot in a saucepan, pour on water to cover and add the wine vinegar. Bring to a simmer, add a pinch of salt and cook for 25 minutes. Leave the beetroot to cool in the water until you are able to handle it, then remove and peel off the skin. Cut the beetroot into 1cm dice, using a sharp knife. Place in a bowl with the sherry vinegar, shallot, garlic and thyme. Season with salt and pepper and drizzle over the olive oil. Mix well and then cover and leave to marinate for at least 2 hours.

Preheat your grill. Lay the bacon on a grill tray and grill on both sides until very crispy. Allow to cool down, then chop the bacon into small pieces.

On a clean board, carefully slice and dice the scallop meat into 5mm pieces. Peel, quarter and core the apple, then cut into 5mm dice. Put the scallops and apple into a bowl with the shallot, gherkin, bacon and chives. Add 2 tsp mayonnaise and mix well. Taste for seasoning and add salt and pepper as required.

To serve, toast the bread on both sides and place on 4 serving plates. Spoon the scallop tartare neatly on top. Spoon some of the marinated beetroot with a little of its dressing alongside. Scatter over the rocket and serve with lemon wedges and the rest of the mayonnaise in a bowl on the side for guests to help themselves.

Scallops and hog's pudding with pear and perry mustard sauce

This is a meal-in-minutes – perfect for a quick lunch. Hog's pudding – a spicy Cornish sausage made from pork, herbs and clotted cream – goes brilliantly with scallops, and the pear cider sauce brings the dish together beautifully. If you don't want a creamy sauce, you can simply omit the cream and reduce the perry a little further to make a vinaigrette instead.

Serves 4

12 large scallops, cleaned (see page 261), corals intact (if preferred) and shells cleaned and retained

1 hog's puddings, skin removed

1 firm, ripe pear

juice of ½ lemon

olive oil for cooking

Cornish sea salt and freshly ground black pepper

Perry mustard sauce

100ml dry perry

50ml double cream

1 tsp wholegrain mustard

200g baby spinach leaves

Put the scallop shells on a tray in a low oven to warm. Cut the hog's pudding into 12 slices. Peel the pear, cut into 5mm dice and toss in the lemon juice to prevent discoloration; set aside.

Place a large non-stick frying pan over a medium heat and add a little olive oil. When hot, add the hog's pudding and cook for 1 minute or until golden. Flip the slices over and then add the scallops, with roes if using. Cook, without moving, for 1 minute until the scallops are golden underneath. Quickly remove the hog's pudding and place on kitchen paper to drain.

Season the scallops and roes with salt and flip them over. Give them another 30 seconds to 1 minute to cook and then transfer to kitchen paper to drain with the hog's pudding; keep warm.

To make the perry mustard sauce, pour the perry into the pan and let bubble to reduce for 2 minutes, then add the cream and simmer for 30 seconds. Stir in the mustard, then add the spinach and cook briefly to wilt.

To serve, spoon the spinach and sauce into the warmed scallop shells and lay the hog's pudding, scallops and diced pear on top. Serve immediately.

The common brown crab is by far our most popular variety, with succulent, tasty flesh that is relatively easy to pick from the shell. The first brown crabs of the season are available to me in late March or early April, when Calum my crab and lobster man puts his pots back out after the rougher winter weather has passed. The larger cock crabs are the first to be caught from the deep. They are around for 8–10 weeks, then like magic, they disappear – often overnight. From July until October, I get the smaller hen crabs, which are just as tasty but don't yield as much meat. Brown crabs will hide out in small caves when the sea is rough and to stay away from predators, but they are pretty awesome predators themselves with strong claws that will grab your fingers if you're not careful. In its youth, a brown crab regularly bursts out of its shell in order to grow a bigger one, leaving it temporarily vulnerable until the soft shell hardens to armour again. Crabs are not easy to catch en masse, which is one reason why UK stocks are pretty good. Pregnant females have to be returned to the sea by law, which also helps a lot. A brown crab is a thing of beauty and should be celebrated when it's about, so treat it with care, cook it simply, savour and enjoy…

If you have ever seen a spider crab walking across the rocks at very low tide, you'll know how fascinating these alien creatures are to watch, and they're very tasty too. From May, they are everywhere for a couple of months, becoming a nuisance to most crab fisherman as they crowd the pots. In low water from a boat, I've seen the seabed almost consumed by spider crabs, as they cover every inch of sand and rock in a breeding frenzy. Then these creatures swim off into the deep, returning the following May in their thousands.

I like to make the most of these tasty crabs in the short time they are available. Towards the end of the season though, you do get the odd one that is watery – a consequence of the crab shedding its shell and devoting its energy to growing a new one. The beginning of the season is really the best time to enjoy them.

Crab

Of the various crabs around our coastline, the one you are most likely to get pinched by is the aggressive, small, fast velvet crab. With its red eyes, super speed and super strength for something so small, it's pretty scary! But, if you want to make a special shellfish soup, these are the crabs to use. They may not yield much in the way of meat, but they have a fantastic flavour, especially when roasted and made into a soup. Unfortunately we don't appreciate them enough and most of the velvet crabs caught in our waters go abroad. Sustainable and around all year, velvet crabs deserve to be eaten more in the UK, though ones with eggs should be avoided.

Shore crabs, the kind we catch on crab lines as kids, are around all year. These are the ones mussel farmers fear the most because they have the capacity to wipe out young mussel beds in a very short time. With negligible meat yield, shore crabs are really only suitable for making stock or soup. But it's well worth doing this as often as you can, as they yield a tasty broth and you'll be doing those mussel farmers a favour…

BEST COOKED
BOILED, SERVED WHOLE AND PICKED
(see page 256)

GARNISHES

SAUCES & DRESSINGS

ACCOMPANIMENTS

ORANGE SEGMENTS

CITRUS MAYONNAISE
(page 108)

CIDER BREAD
(page 235)

CRISPY CAPERS
(page 228)

APPLE AND THYME
DRESSING
(page 68)

BEETROOT AND APPLE
SALAD
(page 150)

WHITE WINE SHALLOTS
(page 231)

HERB EMULSION
(page 86)

CRISPY OYSTERS
(page 34)

Salad of crab, fennel and apple with curried crab mayonnaise

Crab, fennel, apple and curry work so well together that this combination is on one of the restaurant menus more often than not. The flavours really sing together, creating a beautifully balanced dish – an ideal starter or light lunch.

Serves 4

1 live brown crab, about 1 kg, placed in the freezer an hour before cooking (see page 256)

2 tbsp chopped fennel herb or dill

4 tsp white wine shallots (page 231)

2 fennel bulbs, trimmed (outer layer removed)

olive oil for cooking

2 apples

4 handfuls of pea shoots or small salad leaves

Cornish sea salt and freshly ground black pepper

Curried crab mayonnaise

2 egg yolks

brown crabmeat (from above)

finely grated zest and juice of 1 lemon

300ml curry oil (page 227)

To serve

fennel seed bread (page 234), or good-quality bought bread

Bring a large pan of water to the boil (big enough to submerge the crab). Season the water liberally with sea salt to make it as salty as seawater (see page 256). When the water comes to a rolling boil, lower the crab into it and cook for 15 minutes.

Carefully lift the crab out of the water, place on a board and leave until cool enough to handle. Prepare and extract the meat from the crab (as described on page 256), keeping the brown and white meat separate. Blend the brown crabmeat in a food processor until smooth and set aside for the mayonnaise. Pick through the white meat, removing any shell and cartilage; keep cool.

To make the curried crab mayonnaise, whisk the egg yolks, brown crabmeat, lemon zest and juice together in a bowl and slowly add the curry oil, drop by drop to begin with, then in a steady stream, whisking all the time, to make a thick mayonnaise.

Mix the white crabmeat with 3 tbsp of the mayonnaise and season with salt and pepper to taste. Add the fennel herb or dill and half of the white wine shallots. Fork through the crabmeat. Cover and keep cool until ready to serve.

Cut the fennel into 5mm dice. Heat a non-stick frying pan over a medium heat and add a drizzle of olive oil. Add the fennel and cook for 2 minutes without colouring. Transfer to a bowl, season with salt and pepper and allow to cool. Peel, quarter and core the apples and cut into 5mm dice. Add to the fennel with the remaining white wine shallots. Add a drizzle of olive oil and season with salt and pepper.

Preheat your grill or a char-grill. Slice the bread and grill on both sides until well toasted. Place the toast on 4 plates and spoon the crab mayonnaise neatly on top. Arrange the fennel and apple mixture over and around the crab toasts and finish with the pea shoots or salad leaves. Serve at once, with the rest of the mayonnaise in a bowl on the side.

Velvet crab soup with crispy crab cakes

Flavourful 'velvets' work wonderfully for a crab soup, but you can use any variety here, or any other crustacean for that matter. The crab cake served on the soup gives it extra interest but you don't have to make the soup to enjoy these – they are lovely simply with a tasty mayonnaise.

Serves 4

1kg live velvet crabs, placed in the freezer 1 hour before cooking (see page 256)

olive oil for cooking

2 litres water

75g unsalted butter

2 onions, peeled and diced

4 carrots, peeled and sliced

3 garlic cloves, peeled and chopped

1 thyme sprig

finely pared zest of 1 large orange, chopped

1 tarragon sprig

5 ripe plum tomatoes

100ml dry sherry

100ml double cream

Cornish sea salt and freshly ground black pepper

drizzle of orange oil (page 227) to finish

Crab cakes

150g fresh white crabmeat

100g cooked mashed potato

1 shallot, peeled and diced

2 tsp chopped tarragon

2 tsp chopped capers

2 tsp chopped gherkins

50g plain flour

1 egg, beaten

75g Japanese panko breadcrumbs

oil for deep-frying

Preheat the oven to 200°C/Gas 6. Put the velvet crabs in a large roasting tray and drizzle them with olive oil. Roast for 30 minutes and then turn the crabs over and return to the oven for a further 20 minutes. Take the tray from the oven and gradually pour in the water, stirring to deglaze and scraping up the sediment from the bottom.

Place a large saucepan over a medium heat and, when hot, add a good drizzle of olive oil and add the butter. When bubbling, add the onions, carrots, garlic and thyme. Cook, stirring occasionally, for 3 minutes. Next add the orange zest, tarragon and tomatoes and cook for another 5 minutes. Now add the sherry, roasted crabs and all the water. Bring to a simmer and cook gently, uncovered, for 45 minutes, skimming off any impurities that rise to the surface from time to time.

While the soup is cooking, make the crab cakes. Put the picked crabmeat, cooled mashed potato, shallot, tarragon, capers and gherkins into a bowl and mix well. Season with salt and pepper and then shape the mixture into 4 large crab cakes. Chill for 20 minutes to firm up.

Put the flour, beaten egg and breadcrumbs into 3 separate bowls. Take the crab cakes out of the fridge and pass them firstly through the flour, then through the egg and finally through the breadcrumbs. Set aside until serving.

Once the soup is cooked, remove and discard the crab shells, then pour the remaining contents of the pan into a blender. Carefully (as the soup will be hot) blend for 2 minutes, then strain through a fine sieve into a clean pan. Add the cream and bring the soup to a gentle simmer. Taste and correct the seasoning with salt and pepper.

Meanwhile, heat the oil for deep-frying in a deep-fryer or deep, heavy pan to 180°C. Deep-fry the crab cakes for 1 minute until golden and crispy. Drain on kitchen paper and season with salt.

Divide the soup between 4 warmed bowls. Put a hot crispy crab cake in the centre of each portion. Finish with a drizzle of orange oil.

Spider crab, barley and sweetcorn with basil and red onion relish

Spider crabs are only around for a couple of months each year. They always seem to me to be here one minute and gone the next, so make sure you grab the opportunity to enjoy them while you can. Pearl barley and sweetcorn are great vehicles for the crab.

Serves 4

300g spider crabmeat (picked from 2 cooked, live spider crabs, see page 256)

light rapeseed oil for cooking

50g unsalted butter

2 onions, peeled and finely chopped

2 garlic cloves, peeled and finely chopped

100g pearl barley

300ml shellfish stock (page 222)

2 corn-on-the-cobs, kernels cut from the cobs

50g Parmesan, grated

200g spinach leaves, washed

2 tsp chopped basil

Cornish sea salt and freshly ground black pepper

Basil and red onion relish

2 red onions, peeled and finely chopped

1 banana shallot, peeled and finely chopped

200ml red wine

50ml port

1 star anise

100ml good-quality rapeseed or olive oil

2 tsp chopped basil

To finish (optional)

pea shoots

For the basil and red onion relish, put the red onions, shallot, red wine, port and star anise into a saucepan and simmer over a medium heat until the liquid has reduced almost to a syrupy consistency, then set aside to cool.

Meanwhile, heat a large saucepan over a medium heat and add a drizzle of oil and the butter. When hot, add the chopped onions and garlic to the pan and cook for 1 minute. Now add the pearl barley and cook for 2 minutes. Pour in the stock, bring to the boil and cook for 35 minutes, until the liquid has been absorbed and the barley is tender, but with a slight bite.

While the barley is cooking, heat a non-stick frying pan and add a drizzle of oil. When hot, add the sweetcorn kernels and cook for 3 minutes, allowing them to colour and catch at the edges. Remove from the pan, season with salt and pepper and allow to cool.

If the barley isn't quite cooked when the liquid is absorbed, add a little more stock and simmer for a bit longer. Stir in the Parmesan and then add salt and pepper to taste; keep warm.

Add the rapeseed or olive oil to the red onion reduction, stir in the basil and season with salt and pepper; set aside.

Add the spinach and crabmeat to the pearl barley and warm through for 1 minute. Now mix in the sweetcorn, basil and red onion relish, and the chopped basil. Divide between 4 warmed bowls and finish with a scattering of pea shoots if available.

I am extremely lucky to have Port Isaac, one of the best places to source lobster in the UK, only a short drive from my restaurants. Calum, my experienced lobster fisherman, always keep us well stocked from late spring until autumn, with only the best specimens. When you consider that lobsters can live for up to 50 years, they deserve a lot of respect! They certainly get it in our kitchens, as we always cook them with care and simplicity. Their flavour and texture is so good, the less you do to them the better. The lobsters we serve are usually from 8–12 years old and, in my opinion, are at their tastiest at around 600g.

Lobster

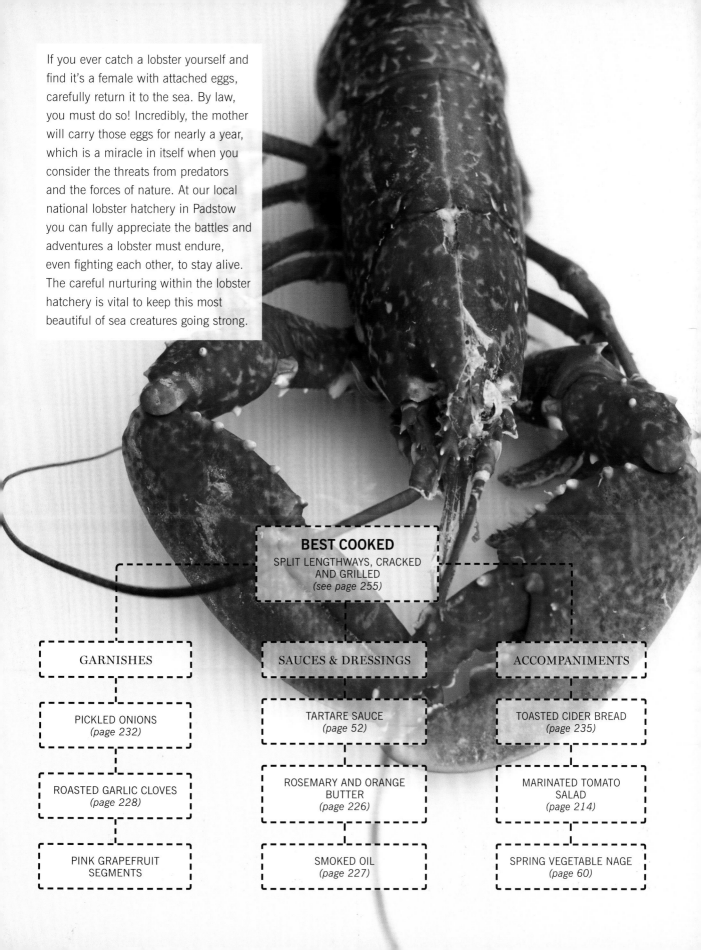

If you ever catch a lobster yourself and find it's a female with attached eggs, carefully return it to the sea. By law, you must do so! Incredibly, the mother will carry those eggs for nearly a year, which is a miracle in itself when you consider the threats from predators and the forces of nature. At our local national lobster hatchery in Padstow you can fully appreciate the battles and adventures a lobster must endure, even fighting each other, to stay alive. The careful nurturing within the lobster hatchery is vital to keep this most beautiful of sea creatures going strong.

BEST COOKED
SPLIT LENGTHWAYS, CRACKED AND GRILLED
(see page 255)

GARNISHES

SAUCES & DRESSINGS

ACCOMPANIMENTS

PICKLED ONIONS
(page 232)

TARTARE SAUCE
(page 52)

TOASTED CIDER BREAD
(page 235)

ROASTED GARLIC CLOVES
(page 228)

ROSEMARY AND ORANGE BUTTER
(page 226)

MARINATED TOMATO SALAD
(page 214)

PINK GRAPEFRUIT SEGMENTS

SMOKED OIL
(page 227)

SPRING VEGETABLE NAGE
(page 60)

Port Isaac lobster risotto with orange and basil

I devised this dish when I opened my first restaurant, as a way of serving the amazing local lobster without putting whole lobsters on the menu, which would have been too expensive for me at the time. For the risotto, I use vegetable stock rather than a stock made from the lobster shells, as it lends a more subtle taste, allowing the flavour of the lobster meat to really shine through.

Serves 4

2 live lobsters, 500–600g each, placed in the freezer 30 minutes before cooking (see page 255)

2 litres vegetable stock (page 222)

50ml olive oil

100g unsalted butter

2 onions, peeled and finely chopped

2 garlic cloves, peeled and crushed

200g Carnaroli risotto rice

8 spring onions, trimmed and finely sliced

100g Parmesan, grated

12 large basil leaves, finely shredded

1 orange, peel and pith removed, segmented and chopped

Cornish sea salt and freshly ground black pepper

Bring a pan of salted water to the boil over a high heat. Once the water is boiling, quickly take the lobsters from the freezer, place on a board and firmly insert the tip of your knife into the cross on the head to kill each one instantly (see page 255). Plunge the lobsters straight into the boiling water and cook them for 8 minutes. Remove from the water and place on a tray to cool down. When cool enough to handle, carefully extract the meat (see page 255). Cover and refrigerate for 1 hour.

Before you start the risotto, chop the lobster meat into equal sized pieces, aiming to get about 20 pieces from each lobster.

To make the risotto, bring the vegetable stock to the boil in a pan and keep it at a gentle simmer. Place a large saucepan over a medium heat and add the olive oil and half of the butter. When the butter is bubbling, add the onions and garlic and cook for 1 minute, without colouring. Next add the rice and cook for 1 minute, stirring all the time. Now add the vegetable stock to the rice a ladleful at a time, stirring and allowing each addition to be absorbed before adding the next. Cook the rice in this way for 14 minutes or until it is *al dente* and you have a creamy looking risotto.

Now turn the heat down to its lowest setting. Add the chopped lobster and spring onions to the rice and cook for 1 minute. Then add the Parmesan, remaining butter (in pieces) and the basil. Warm gently for 2 minutes, stirring all the time. Finally add the chopped orange and season with salt and pepper to taste. Serve straight away.

Lobster cocktail with oven-dried cherry tomatoes

If you are having a dinner party and you want to impress, this unique combination will fit the bill. The brioche has a great flavour and marries so well with the fresh lobster and sweet acidity of the cherry tomatoes. Taking classics to a new level is one of my favourite ways of creating new dishes, and this is one of them.

Serves 4

2 live lobsters, about 800g each, placed in the freezer 30 minutes before cooking (see page 255)

2 tbsp mayonnaise (page 225)

1 tbsp tomato ketchup (page 233), or use ready-made

2 tsp chopped tarragon

2 baby gem lettuces, leaves separated and washed

Cornish sea salt and freshly ground black pepper

Oven-dried cherry tomatoes

16 cherry tomatoes

basil oil (page 227) or olive oil to drizzle

1 shallot, peeled and chopped

1 garlic clove, peeled and chopped

2 tsp red wine vinegar

To serve

tarragon brioche (page 235), or good-quality bought brioche

Bring a pan of salted water to the boil over a high heat. Once the water is boiling, quickly take the lobsters from the freezer, place on a board and firmly insert the tip of your knife into the cross on the head to kill each one instantly (see page 255). Plunge the lobsters straight into the boiling water and cook them for 11 minutes. Remove from the water and place on a tray to cool down. When cool enough to handle, carefully extract the meat (see page 255). Cover and refrigerate for 1 hour.

For the oven-dried tomatoes, preheat the oven for 160°C/Gas 3. Halve the cherry tomatoes. Line a shallow roasting tray with foil, drizzle with basil or olive oil and sprinkle with salt and pepper. Arrange the cherry tomatoes, cut side up, in a single layer on the tray and sprinkle with the shallot and garlic. Drizzle with the wine vinegar and a little more oil. Place in the oven for 30 minutes until the tomatoes are lightly roasted and slightly dried. Set aside to cool.

To make the cocktail, chop the lobster into 1cm pieces. Put the mayonnaise, tomato ketchup and chopped tarragon into a bowl and mix well. Add the lobster pieces and mix carefully. Season with salt and pepper to taste.

Put the lettuce leaves and roasted tomatoes into a bowl and dress with the juices and oil from the tomatoes' roasting tray. Preheat a griddle, if you have one, or the grill, and toast the brioche on both sides. Drizzle with a little olive oil and place a slice of toast on each serving plate. Pile the lobster cocktail on top. Arrange the lettuce and tomatoes on the plates and serve.

Squid & cuttlefish

These cephalopods are loosely classified as shellfish as they have an internal shell – squid has a quill, while cuttlefish has a cuttlebone. Squid is a fascinating creature – the ultimate hunting machine. It shoots through the water, steered by its large fins, and siphons water through its body to create what can only be described as jet power. It can change colour to match its surroundings, switch direction in the water instantly, and shoot ink into the path of any prey or predator to cause confusion. Squid is very sustainable, aided by a fast life cycle – it has only a one-year breeding season. Just avoid eating it fresh during winter and early spring, when it is spawning. When you buy squid, check that the body and tentacles have no signs of pinkness, which indicate that it is old. In my experience, frozen squid is often more tender than fresh, because the freezing process helps to tenderise the flesh.

My budgie learnt to appreciate cuttlefish long before I tried it. When I was a kid, 'Burt' the budgie always had a cuttlebone in his cage to keep his beak busy. Now I can see what the fuss was all about. This cephalopod is probably one of the most intelligent creatures in the sea. Like squid, camouflage is one of its most impressive attributes, enabling it to blend into any situation, whether hiding or hunting. But unlike squid, which I prefer to cook quickly, I enjoy cuttlefish slow cooked or braised.

I am also a big fan of cuttlefish ink, which has more flavour than squid ink and there is always more of it. Cuttlefish live for a few years and breed inshore, where most of them are caught. They should be avoided during the spring and early summer spawning season. One of our local fishermen once brought me a cuttlefish that had got caught in his lobster pot. Not realising it was live, I grabbed it and got a nasty clip from its beak… I certainly wouldn't want to be a fish engaged in battle with a cuttlefish.

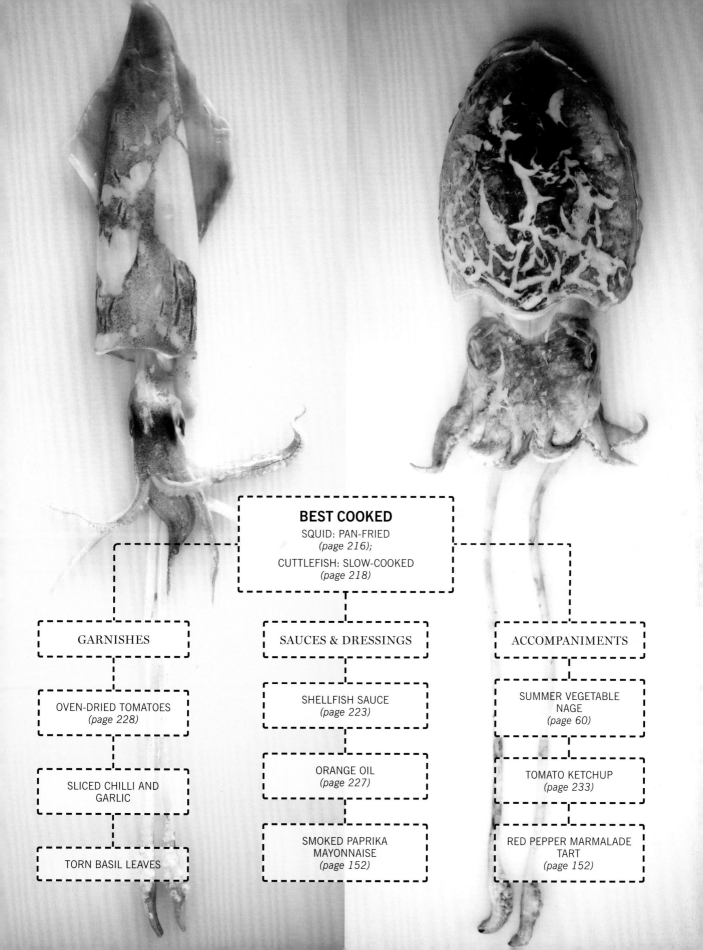

BEST COOKED
SQUID: PAN-FRIED
(page 216);

CUTTLEFISH: SLOW-COOKED
(page 218)

GARNISHES

OVEN-DRIED TOMATOES
(page 228)

SLICED CHILLI AND
GARLIC

TORN BASIL LEAVES

SAUCES & DRESSINGS

SHELLFISH SAUCE
(page 223)

ORANGE OIL
(page 227)

SMOKED PAPRIKA
MAYONNAISE
(page 152)

ACCOMPANIMENTS

SUMMER VEGETABLE
NAGE
(page 60)

TOMATO KETCHUP
(page 233)

RED PEPPER MARMALADE
TART
(page 152)

Crispy squid, marinated tomato salad and lemon and chilli mayonnaise

This simple recipe can be prepared quickly and is one of the nicest ways of eating squid. I like to serve it as a big family-style dish for all to share. It is adaptable too – change the salad or flavour the mayonnaise differently if you like. The most important thing is to make sure the squid is really crispy.

Serves 4

4 squid, 150–200g each, cleaned and cut into rings, tentacles reserved (see page 262)

100g plain flour to dust

1 tsp smoked paprika

1 tsp ground cumin

oil for deep-frying

Cornish sea salt and freshly ground black pepper

Marinated tomato salad

4 plum tomatoes

2 beef tomatoes

12 cherry tomatoes

2 shallots, peeled and diced

2 garlic cloves, peeled and finely chopped

1 tsp chopped thyme

1 tsp chopped oregano

olive oil to drizzle

Lemon and chilli mayonnaise

3 egg yolks

1 tsp English mustard

1 red Dutch chilli, deseeded and finely chopped

finely grated zest and juice of 1 lemon

2 tsp chopped flat-leaf parsley

200ml light olive oil

To serve

lemon wedges

First prepare the marinated tomato salad. Slice the plum and beef tomatoes and halve the cherry tomatoes. Place them all in a large bowl. Add the shallots, garlic, thyme and oregano and season the tomatoes well with salt and pepper. Drizzle over some olive oil and mix together with your hands. Lay the tomatoes out neatly on a large serving plate or platter and leave to marinate for 1 hour before serving.

To make the mayonnaise, put the egg yolks, mustard, chilli and lemon zest and juice in a food processor and blend together for 30 seconds. With the motor running, slowly add the olive oil in a steady stream until you have a nice, thick mayonnaise. Season with salt and pepper to taste. Add the chopped parsley and blend again for 30 seconds. Transfer the mayonnaise to a tub and refrigerate until you want to serve it.

When ready to serve, put the flour into a large bowl with the smoked paprika, cumin and a pinch of salt, and mix together well. Heat the oil in a deep-fryer or other suitable deep, heavy pan to 180°C. When the oil is hot, cook the squid in batches. Pass through the seasoned flour, pat off any excess, then carefully add to the oil. Fry the squid for 1–2 minutes until crispy. Drain on kitchen paper and keep warm while you cook the rest.

Serve immediately, with the tomato salad, mayonnaise and lemon wedges.

Squid with pork belly, satsuma, fennel and squid ink mayonnaise

You might be sceptical about this combination but pork belly is lovely with squid, and with cuttlefish too. Bacon goes well with most seafood and here the cured and slow-cooked pork belly is crisped up until it's almost like bacon. Fennel and satsuma marry perfectly and the squid ink mayonnaise brings all the flavours together beautifully.

Serves 4

2 squid, about 200g each, cleaned and cut into rings, tentacles reserved (see page 262)

1.5kg pork belly, skin and bones removed

100g fine sea salt

100g caster sugar

4 tbsp fennel seeds

light rapeseed oil for cooking

100ml good-quality orange juice

1 fennel bulb, trimmed and quartered

2 satsumas, peel and pith removed, segmented

Cornish sea salt and freshly ground black pepper

Squid ink mayonnaise

3 egg yolks

1 tsp English mustard

2 tbsp white wine vinegar

3 tsp squid or cuttlefish ink

200ml light olive oil

Lay the pork belly on a roasting tray. Put the salt, sugar and fennel seeds in a food processor and blitz for 1 minute. Rub the salt mix into the meat all over and leave to cure in the fridge for 4 hours.

Preheat the oven to 200°C/Gas 6. Wash the cure off the pork belly and pat the meat dry. Drizzle a little oil over the meat and roast for 40 minutes, then lower the oven setting to 100°C/Gas ¼. Roast for a further 2 hours or until the pork is cooked through. Allow to cool, then place in the fridge to firm up.

Bring the orange juice to a simmer in a saucepan over a medium heat. Let bubble until reduced by half, then add the fennel and a pinch of salt. Simmer for 20 minutes until the fennel is soft, but not overcooked. Remove the fennel with a slotted spoon and set aside to cool on a plate. Continue to simmer the orange juice until reduced to a syrup consistency. Check the seasoning and put to one side.

To make the squid ink mayonnaise, put the egg yolks, mustard, wine vinegar and squid or cuttlefish ink in a food processor and blend for 30 seconds. With the motor running, slowly add the olive oil in a steady stream until you have a nice, thick mayonnaise. Season with salt and pepper to taste. Transfer the mayonnaise to a tub and refrigerate until you want to serve it.

To finish the dish, heat the oven to 200°C/Gas 6. Cut the pork belly into twelve 3cm cubes and lay these on an oiled roasting tray with the fennel quarters. Heat in the oven for 10 minutes.

Meanwhile, heat a non-stick frying pan over a medium heat. When the pan is hot, add a drizzle of oil. Season the squid with salt and pepper and carefully place it in the hot pan. Cook for 1 minute until lightly coloured, turning once, then remove from the pan and drain on kitchen paper.

Remove the pork and fennel from the oven and divide between warmed plates. Arrange the squid and satsuma segments on each plate. Finally spoon on some of the ink mayonnaise and add a drizzle of the orange and fennel syrup. Serve at once, with the remaining mayonnaise in a bowl on the side.

Warm salad of cuttlefish and asparagus with cuttlefish ink dressing

When it's in season, we get a lot of cuttlefish in Cornwall and I love cooking with it. Unfortunately, it's not very popular in the UK and most of the cuttlefish caught around our shores goes abroad, which is a real shame as it's a great sustainable British seafood.

Serves 4

1kg cuttlefish, cleaned and left whole, ink reserved

olive oil for cooking

1 onion, peeled and roughly chopped

2 carrots, peeled and chopped

4 garlic cloves, peeled and crushed

6 ripe tomatoes, cut into quarters

100ml dry white wine

600ml roast fish stock (page 222)

2 shallots, peeled and finely chopped

75ml red wine vinegar

1 tbsp cuttlefish ink (see above)

150ml extra virgin olive oil

16 asparagus spears, lower part of stems peeled

20g fine capers

4 tarragon sprigs, leaves only

squeeze of lemon juice

Cornish sea salt and freshly ground black pepper

Heat a large saucepan over a medium heat and add a drizzle of olive oil. Add the onion, carrots and garlic and sweat for 3 minutes, stirring occasionally. Add the tomatoes and cook for another 3 minutes.

Add the wine and let bubble to reduce right down, then add the fish stock. Bring to a simmer, add the cuttlefish and simmer very gently for 1½ hours or until tender. When the cuttlefish is ready, remove it from the stock with a slotted spoon and leave to cool. Strain the stock, cool and reserve 100ml for the dressing.

For the dressing, in a bowl combine the shallots, wine vinegar and the 100ml reserved cuttlefish stock and leave to stand for 30 minutes. Whisk the cuttlefish ink into the extra virgin olive oil and then whisk this into the shallot mixture. Season with salt to taste.

Bring a large pan of salted water to the boil and blanch the asparagus for 2 minutes. (If you're doing this ahead, refresh in iced water.)

When cool, cut the cuttlefish into 2cm strips. Gently warm these in some of the dressing (don't let it get too hot). Place the asparagus, capers and tarragon in a large bowl and gently mix with the warm cuttlefish. Add a squeeze of lemon juice and season with salt and pepper to taste.

Serve the salad in warmed bowls or soup plates with the rest of the dressing in a jug on the side and some crusty bread.

Base
recipes

Stocks

Roast fish stock

Makes about 500ml

1kg turbot, brill or sole bones, washed and all blood removed

water to cover

Preheat your oven to 200°C/Gas 6. Line a roasting tray with silicone paper and lay the fish bones on it. Roast for 30 minutes, then turn the bones over and roast for another 10 minutes. Transfer the roasted bones to a stockpot and pour on enough water to cover. Bring to a simmer over a medium heat and skim off any impurities from the surface. Simmer for 30 minutes, then take off the heat and strain through a sieve into another pan. Bring the stock back to a simmer and reduce by half. Remove from the heat and allow to cool. The stock is now ready to use. You can store it the fridge for up to 3 days or freeze it for up to 2 months.

Meat stock

Makes about 300ml

2kg veal bones

1kg lamb bones

75cl bottle red wine

water to cover

Preheat your oven to 200°C/Gas 6. Place all the bones in a roasting tray and roast for 30 minutes, then turn them over and roast for another 30 minutes. Transfer the bones to a stockpot and cover with the wine and water. Bring to the boil and simmer for 6 hours, skimming the surface regularly. Pass the stock through a sieve into another pan. Bring back to a simmer and reduce by three-quarters until it starts to thicken. Remove from the heat and allow to cool. The stock is now ready to use. You can store it in the fridge for up to 3 days or freeze it for up to 2 months.

Shellfish stock

Makes about 500ml

1kg frozen shell-on prawns

olive oil for cooking

2 onions, peeled and chopped

3 carrots, peeled and chopped

6 ripe tomatoes, chopped

6 garlic cloves, peeled and chopped

finely pared zest and juice of 1 orange

water to cover

Preheat your oven to 200°C/Gas 6. Put the frozen prawns on a roasting tray and roast for 30 minutes. Meanwhile, heat a large pan over a medium heat, add a little olive oil and sweat the onions, carrots, tomatoes, garlic and orange zest for 5 minutes until lightly coloured. Once the prawns are roasted, chop them and add to the pan. Pour on enough water to cover and add the orange juice. Bring to a simmer and simmer for 1 hour. Strain through a sieve into another pan. Simmer to reduce by half. Remove from the heat and allow to cool. The stock is now ready to use. You can store it in the fridge for up to 2 days or freeze it for up to a month.

Crab stock Replace the prawns with 1kg live shore crabs and roast them for an extra 15 minutes.

Vegetable stock

Makes about 2 litres

2 onions, peeled and finely chopped

6 carrots, peeled and finely chopped

6 celery sticks, finely chopped

2 leeks, trimmed, washed and finely sliced

2 garlic cloves, peeled and crushed

10 white peppercorns

2 star anise

2 tsp fennel seeds

pinch of sea salt

water to cover

500ml dry white wine

1 thyme sprig

handful of parsley stalks

Put all of the vegetables, the garlic, spices and salt into a large saucepan and pour on enough water to cover. Bring to a simmer over a medium heat. Simmer for 30 minutes and then remove from the heat. Pour the wine into the stock and add the herbs. Leave to cool. For best results, leave overnight in the fridge before straining the stock to remove the vegetables, spices and herbs. Your stock is now ready to use. It can be frozen for up to 2 months.

Sauces & dressings

Lemon sauce

Makes about 350ml

1 egg yolk

finely grated zest and juice of 1 lemon

200ml light olive oil

50ml double cream

100ml roast fish stock (see page 222)

Cornish sea salt

Whisk the egg yolk, lemon zest and lemon juice together in a bowl for 1 minute and then slowly whisk in the olive oil, as for a mayonnaise. Season with salt to taste. (You can make the sauce ahead to this stage and keep it in the fridge for up to 3 days.) To finish the sauce, whisk in the cream, followed by the fish stock. To serve, gently warm the sauce over a medium heat; do not allow to boil, or the sauce will curdle. If the sauce is too thick, add a little more fish stock to thin it down. Taste and season with a little more salt if required. Serve immediately.

Red wine sauce

Makes about 300ml

100g caster sugar

3 banana shallots, peeled and chopped

6 garlic cloves, peeled and crushed

1 thyme sprig

100ml red wine vinegar

500ml red wine

500ml meat stock (see page 222)

Heat a small heavy-based pan over a medium heat and add the sugar. After about 2 minutes, when the sugar has melted and started to caramelise, add the shallots, garlic and thyme. Cook, stirring, for 2 minutes to soften, then add the wine vinegar and reduce for 2 minutes. Pour in the wine and reduce until the liquor looks syrupy. Finally add the meat stock and let the sauce bubble to reduce until it is thick enough to coat the back of a spoon. Serve at once, or allow the sauce to cool and refrigerate for up to 5 days, or freeze.

Saffron sauce

Makes about 200ml

750ml roast fish stock (see page 222)

250ml shellfish stock (see page 222)

4 ripe tomatoes

2 tarragon sprigs

50g unsalted butter

½ tsp saffron strands

Cornish sea salt

Put all the ingredients into a saucepan. Bring to a simmer and simmer until the stock has reduced down to about 200ml. Transfer the mixture to a blender and blitz for 3 minutes. It will emulsify into a thick sauce. Taste and add a little salt if needed. Serve straight away.

Shellfish sauce

Makes about 300ml

750ml roast fish stock (see page 222)

250ml shellfish stock (see page 222)

5 ripe tomatoes, chopped

5 tarragon sprigs

pinch of saffron strands

50g unsalted butter

Cornish sea salt and freshly ground black pepper

Pour both stocks into a large saucepan and add the tomatoes, tarragon, saffron and butter. Bring to a simmer and let bubble until reduced to about 200ml. Tip the contents of the pan into a blender and blitz for 4 minutes. This will emulsify everything together, resulting in a velvety sauce. Taste for seasoning, adding salt and pepper as required. Serve straight away or, if preparing ahead, allow to cool and heat through to serve.

Horseradish sauce

Makes about 300ml

200ml vegetable stock (see page 222)

50ml double cream

200ml semi-skimmed milk

50g creamed horseradish, or to taste

Cornish sea salt and freshly ground pepper

In a pan, bring the vegetable stock to a simmer and reduce to 3 tbsp. Add the cream and milk and season with salt and pepper. Bring the sauce to 80°C (below simmering) and froth with a hand-held stick blender or whisk. Add the creamed horseradish to taste. Before serving, bring back to 80°C and froth again.

Piccalilli sauce

Makes about 150ml

1 tsp cayenne pepper

1 tsp ground ginger

1 tbsp ground turmeric

1 tbsp mustard seeds

2 garlic cloves, peeled and chopped

1 tbsp English mustard

100g caster sugar

200ml white wine vinegar

200ml water

250ml roast fish stock (see page 222)

250ml shellfish stock (see page 222)

50g unsalted butter

1 shallot, peeled and chopped

1 leek, trimmed, washed and finely sliced

Cornish sea salt

Put all the spices into a small, dry frying pan and toast over a medium heat for 1 minute. Add the garlic, mustard, ½ tsp salt, sugar, wine vinegar and water. Let bubble until well reduced and syrupy. In another pan, bring both stocks to a simmer and whisk in the butter. Now stir in the spiced reduction. Add the shallot and leek and simmer for about 10 minutes until the liquid has reduced by three-quarters. Blitz in a blender for about 2 minutes until smooth, then pass through a sieve.

English mustard dressing

Makes about 350ml

1 banana shallot, peeled and finely chopped

1 garlic clove, peeled and finely chopped

2 tsp English mustard

4 tsp white wine vinegar or cider vinegar

300ml sunflower oil

Cornish sea salt and freshly ground black pepper

Put the shallot, garlic, mustard and vinegar into a bowl. Whisk together for 1 minute and then slowly add the oil, whisking all the time. Once the oil is all incorporated, season with salt and pepper to taste.

Parsley, lemon and garlic dressing

Makes about 225ml

1 head of garlic, broken into cloves (unpeeled)

250ml light rapeseed oil

handful of flat-leaf parsley leaves

finely pared zest of 1 lemon, plus a squeeze of juice

Cornish sea salt and freshly ground black pepper

Put the garlic cloves into a saucepan, pour on the oil and place over a low heat. Bring gently to just below a simmer. Let it tick over at this temperature for 1 hour, with just the odd bubble breaking the surface now and again. Take off the heat and add the parsley and lemon zest. Cover and leave overnight to infuse.

To serve, warm the infused oil and season with salt, pepper and a squeeze of lemon juice to taste. Strain the dressing before using.

Roasted garlic, olive and gherkin dressing

Makes about 200ml

1 head of garlic
rapeseed oil to drizzle
150g unsalted butter
1 shallot, peeled and chopped
100ml Noilly Prat or dry vermouth
1 gherkin, finely chopped
6 green olives, finely chopped
Cornish sea salt

Heat your oven to 200°C/Gas 6. Lay a piece of foil on your work surface and sprinkle with 1 tsp salt. Place the garlic bulb in the middle and drizzle with a little rapeseed oil. Wrap the garlic in the foil, place the parcel on a tray and bake for 20 minutes. When cool enough to handle, peel and chop the flesh.

Melt the butter in a saucepan over a medium heat. Continue to heat until the butter turns nut brown and then immediately remove from the heat.

Heat a second pan over a medium heat. Add a drizzle of oil, then the shallot and chopped roasted garlic and cook for 1 minute, without colouring. Add the Noilly Prat and let bubble to reduce to about 2 tbsp liquid. Add the gherkin and olives and remove from the heat. Add 8 tbsp of the brown butter to the mixture and mix well. To serve, warm through but do not allow to boil.

Pickled walnut dressing

Makes 300ml

2 shallots, peeled and finely chopped
75g pickled walnuts, chopped, plus 75ml vinegar from jar
75ml extra virgin olive oil
75ml walnut oil
Cornish sea salt

Put the shallots, pickled walnuts and vinegar into a bowl and leave to stand for 30 minutes. Whisk in the olive and walnut oils and season with salt to taste.

Mayonnaise

Makes about 350ml

3 egg yolks
1 tsp English mustard
juice of ½ lemon or 2 tsp white wine vinegar or cider vinegar
300ml light rapeseed oil
Cornish sea salt and freshly ground black pepper

Put the egg yolks, mustard and lemon juice or wine vinegar into a bowl and whisk together for 1 minute. Now slowly add the oil, drop by drop to begin with, then in a steady stream, whisking constantly, until the mixture is emulsified and thick.

Alternatively, you can make the mayonnaise in a blender or food processor, blending the egg yolks, mustard and lemon juice or vinegar for 1 minute and then adding the oil slowly through the funnel with the motor running.

Season the mayonnaise with salt and pepper to taste. Cover and refrigerate until ready to serve. It will keep in the fridge for a couple of days.

Variations I use various different flavoured mayonnaises to complement dishes and you'll find most of these within the main fish recipes. They can also be mixed and matched with other fish dishes. These are my favourites:

Basic herb mayonnaise Add 3–4 tbsp chopped herbs of your choice to the finished mayonnaise. Dill, tarragon and/or parsley are the best options with fish.

Cheddar and chive mayonnaise Use cider vinegar and blend 25g finely grated Cheddar with the mayonnaise base. Once the oil is all incorporated, add 3–4 tbsp chopped chives.

Citrus mayonnaise (see page 108)
Curried crab mayonnaise (see page 200)
Horseradish mayonnaise (see page 168)
Lemon and chilli mayonnaise (see page 214)
Oyster mayonnaise (see page 190)
Smoked paprika mayonnaise (see page 152)
Squid ink mayonnaise (see page 216)
Tarragon mayonnaise (see page 38)
Tartare sauce (see page 52)

Flavoured butters & oils

Parsley and garlic butter

Makes about 200g

200g salted butter, softened

4 garlic cloves, peeled and finely chopped

3 tbsp chopped parsley

freshly ground black pepper

Put the butter, garlic, parsley and some pepper in a food processor or blender and process for 2 minutes until well blended. Lay a sheet of cling film on a work surface and spoon the butter onto it. Wrap the butter in the cling film, rolling it into a long sausage, and tie the ends of the cling film to secure. Chill for 2 hours before serving. The butter will keep in the fridge for a week, or it can be frozen.

Anchovy and tarragon butter

Makes about 200g

200g unsalted butter, softened

4 salted anchovy fillets

5 tsp chopped tarragon

20 anchovy fillets in olive oil

Cornish sea salt and freshly ground black pepper

Put the butter, salted anchovies and 4 tsp of the chopped tarragon in a food processor or blender and add some salt and pepper. Process for 2 minutes until well blended. Lay a sheet of cling film on a work surface and spoon the butter onto it. Wrap the butter in the cling film, rolling it into a long sausage, and tie the ends of the cling film to secure. Chill for 2 hours.

To serve, place the flavoured butter in a pan and warm through gently; do not allow to boil. Add the final teaspoon of tarragon and the marinated anchovy fillets.

Note This is also very good spooned over potatoes for an unusual potato salad.

Rosemary and orange butter

Makes about 250g

2 tbsp chopped rosemary

1 shallot, peeled and chopped

2 garlic cloves, peeled and chopped

finely grated zest of 1 orange

250g unsalted butter, softened

Cornish sea salt and freshly ground black pepper

Put the chopped rosemary, shallot, garlic and orange zest into a bowl. Add the softened butter and mix together with a spatula until evenly blended. Season with salt and pepper to taste. Lay a sheet of cling film on a work surface and spoon the butter onto it. Wrap the butter in the cling film, rolling it into a long sausage, and tie the ends of the cling film to secure. Chill for 2 hours before using.

Potted clam or cockle butter

Makes about 250g

250g unsalted butter, softened

4 tsp chopped curly parsley

20 rasps of nutmeg

1 tsp cayenne pepper

finely grated zest and juice of 1 lemon

2 shallots, peeled and finely chopped

1 garlic clove, peeled and finely chopped

500g–1kg (or more) cockles or clams, cooked (see page 178)

Cornish sea salt and freshly ground black pepper

Put the butter, parsley, nutmeg, cayenne, lemon zest and juice in a food processor or blender and process for 2 minutes until well blended. Transfer to a bowl and mix in the shallots, garlic and salt to taste. Lay a sheet of cling film on a work surface and spoon the butter onto it. Wrap the butter in the cling film, rolling it into a long sausage, and tie the ends of the cling film to secure. Chill for 2 hours to firm up before serving. The butter will keep in the fridge for a week, or it can be frozen.

To serve, place the flavoured butter in a pan and warm through gently; do not allow to boil. Add the cockles or clams and warm through gently.

Lemon oil

Makes about 400ml
finely pared zest of 4 unwaxed lemons
300ml light rapeseed oil
100ml light olive oil

Put all of the ingredients into a blender and blitz for 2 minutes. Pour the oil mixture into a jug and leave to infuse and settle for 24 hours. Decant the oil into another container. Keep in the fridge and use within a month.

Orange oil

Makes about 400ml
finely pared zest of 4 oranges
300ml light rapeseed oil
100ml light olive oil

Put all of the ingredients into a blender and blitz for 2 minutes. Pour the oil mixture into a jug and leave to infuse and settle for 24 hours. Decant the oil into another container. Keep in the fridge and use within a month.

Basil oil

Makes about 150ml
30g basil leaves
30g flat-leaf parsley leaves
150ml light olive oil
Cornish sea salt

Bring a pan of salted water to a simmer and get a bowl of iced water ready. When the water is simmering, add the herbs and blanch for 30 seconds. Immediately scoop out the herbs and plunge them straight into the iced water to cool quickly. Drain and squeeze out all excess water. Put the blanched herbs into a blender with the olive oil and blitz for 2 minutes. Transfer the mixture to a container and refrigerate for at least 3–4 hours, preferably overnight.

Warm the oil slightly and then pass it through a sieve into a clean container. The oil is now ready to use. It will keep in the fridge for 1 week.

Smoked paprika oil

Makes about 250ml
2 tsp smoked paprika
250ml rapeseed oil

Sprinkle the smoked paprika into a dry frying pan and toast over a medium heat for 1–2 minutes until it releases its aroma. Remove from the heat and add the oil. Leave to infuse for 24 hours. Decant into a glass jar. This oil can be stored in a fridge for about 3 months.

Curry oil

Makes about 400ml
4 tsp mild curry powder
400ml light rapeseed oil

Sprinkle the curry powder into a dry frying pan and toast over a medium heat for 1–2 minutes until it releases its aroma; don't let it burn. Pour the oil into the pan and remove from the heat. Give it a good stir and then pour it into a jug. Leave to infuse and settle for 24 hours, then decant the curry oil into another container. It will keep for 3 months in a dark cupboard.

Smoked oil

Makes about 200ml
200ml sunflower oil
100g natural oak chippings

Pour the oil into a metal bowl that will fit into an old saucepan. Heat the saucepan and add the oak chippings. When the chippings start to smoke, set the bowl of oil in the pan and cover it with a cold damp tea-towel. Lower the heat and allow to smoke for 40 minutes, re-cooling the tea-towel in cold water four times during this period. Remove the pan from the heat and leave covered until cold. Lift the bowl of oil from the pan and decant into a bottle.

Garnishes & vegetables

Oven-dried tomatoes

Serves 6

8 ripe plum tomatoes
2 garlic cloves, peeled and sliced
2 thyme sprigs, picked and chopped
100ml olive oil
caster sugar to taste
Cornish sea salt and freshly ground
black pepper

Heat your oven to 110°C/Gas ¼. Bring a large pan of salted water to a simmer on a medium heat. Immerse the tomatoes in the water for 20 seconds and then remove with a slotted spoon and plunge straight into a bowl of iced water to cool quickly. Take out the tomatoes and peel away the skins.

Cut the tomatoes lengthways into quarters. Using a small knife, cut out the core and seeds and lay the tomatoes cut side up on a foil-lined tray. Sprinkle over the garlic, thyme and olive oil, then season with salt, pepper and sugar. Place in the oven for 1 hour, then turn the tomatoes over and cook for a further 45 minutes.

If not using straight away, layer the tomatoes in a tub or jar and cover with olive oil. They will keep in the fridge for up to a week.

Crispy capers

Makes 4 tsp

4 tsp large capers, drained
oil for deep-frying
Cornish sea salt

Pat the capers dry with kitchen paper. Heat a 3cm depth of oil in a suitable pan to 180°C. Drop the capers into the hot oil and deep-fry for 1 minute until crispy. Drain on kitchen paper and sprinkle with a little salt.

Roasted garlic

Makes 2–3 tbsp

1 large head of garlic
olive oil to drizzle
Cornish sea salt

Heat your oven to 200°C/Gas 6. Lay a piece of foil on your work surface and sprinkle with 1 tsp salt. Place the garlic bulb in the middle and drizzle with a little olive oil. Wrap in the foil and place the parcel on a baking tray. Bake for 20 minutes until the cloves are soft. Leave until they are cool enough to handle, then peel off the skin and chop or mash the flesh.

Roasted garlic cloves You can roast cloves individually on a baking tray at 200°C/Gas 6 for 15–20 minutes to use as a garnish.

Roasted garlic purée Blitz the garlic pulp in a small blender until smooth. You can store the purée in a small jar covered with a thin film of olive oil in the fridge for up to a month.

Crispy seaweed

Serves 4

4 large handfuls of seaweed (ideally gutweed), well washed, or finely sliced greens or Savoy cabbage
oil for deep-frying
Cornish sea salt

To cook the seaweed, heat the oil in a deep-fryer or other deep, heavy pan to 200°C. Dry the seaweed (or greens) thoroughly by squeezing in a tea towel or cloth to remove all water. Deep-fry in the hot oil in small batches for 2 minutes until crispy. Drain on kitchen paper and season with a little salt. Serve hot.

Lemon and tarragon stuffing

Serves 4

5 slices of white bread

25g tarragon

grated zest of ½ lemon

2 tbsp olive oil

Cornish sea salt and freshly ground
black pepper

Tear the bread into chunks and put into a food processor
with the tarragon, lemon zest, olive oil and some salt and
pepper. Process until the bread is reduced to crumbs and
the ingredients are well combined.

Use to stuff butterflied and pin-boned fish, such as
sardines or small red mullet. Lay the stuffing on the flesh
side and bring the edges together to re-form the fish to
its natural shape. Secure with kitchen string and bake in
a preheated oven at 200°C/Gas 6 for 8 minutes.

Cheddar rarebit

Serves 6

325g full-flavoured Cheddar (ideally
Davidstow), grated

60ml Sharp's Doom Bar beer (or other
bitter)

30g plain flour

25g white breadcrumbs

1 tsp English mustard

3 egg yolks

Cornish sea salt and freshly ground black
pepper

Put the cheese and beer in a saucepan and heat gently
until the cheese melts and starts to bubble. Add the flour
and cook, stirring, for 1 minute. Remove from the heat and
add the breadcrumbs, mustard, egg yolks and seasoning.
Mix well, then allow to cool.

Top chunky cod or pollack portions with the rarebit
mixture and bake in a preheated oven at 200°C/Gas 6 for
12–15 minutes, depending on the thickness of the fish.
Serve immediately, with roasted baby vine tomatoes.

Cheddar and parsley crust

Serves 4

75g fresh white breadcrumbs

4 tbsp grated full-flavoured Cheddar
(ideally Davidstow)

4 tbsp chopped parsley

1 tbsp chopped dill

1 garlic clove, peeled and finely chopped

25g butter, melted

rapeseed oil to drizzle

Cornish sea salt and freshly ground black
pepper

Put the breadcrumbs, grated cheese, parsley, dill, garlic
and some seasoning into a bowl. Add the butter and mix
well, using a fork.

Divide the crumb mixture between white fish fillets,
such as cod or haddock, pressing it on top of each piece
in a thick, even layer. Drizzle over a little rapeseed oil and
bake in a preheated oven at 200°C/Gas 6 for 10–12
minutes until the crust is crisp and lightly golden and the
fish is just cooked through.

Potato, garlic and herb dumplings

Serves 4

300g potato, baked until tender

1 garlic bulb, roasted whole and puréed (see page 228)

1½ tbsp grated Parmesan

1 egg yolk

65g 'OO' flour (pasta flour)

2 tsp lemon oil or olive oil

2 tbsp fine capers in vinegar, finely chopped

3 tbsp chopped flat-leaf parsley, chervil or other herbs

light rapeseed oil for cooking

Cornish sea salt and freshly ground black pepper

Peel the potato and pass through a ricer or drum sieve into a bowl. Add the garlic, Parmesan and egg yolk and lightly fold together in a bowl; avoid overworking as this would make your dumplings tough and heavy. Lightly fold in the flour, oil, capers and parsley or chervil. Season with salt and pepper.

Bring a large pan of water to the boil, salt well and add a little oil. Have ready a bowl of iced water. Turn the dough out onto a floured surface and shape into small balls, the size of marbles. Blanch in the boiling water, in batches if necessary, until the dumplings come to the surface, about 2 minutes. Transfer to the iced water to cool quickly. Once cold, dry on a tea towel.

Unless serving straight away, gently toss the dumplings in a little oil in a container to stop them sticking together. They will keep in the fridge for a few days.

To serve, heat a non-stick frying pan and add a drizzle of oil. Fry the dumplings in the hot oil for about 3 minutes until they are lightly golden brown all over. Drain on kitchen paper and serve.

Wild garlic dumplings Omit the roasted garlic, capers and parsley. Add 4 tbsp chopped wild garlic to the mixture with the Parmesan and season with salt.

Braised haricot beans

Serves 4

200g dried haricot beans

rapeseed oil for cooking

1 shallot, peeled

2 garlic cloves, peeled

1 carrot, peeled

1 celery stick

2 bay leaves

1 rosemary sprig

about 600ml water or roast fish stock (see page 222)

Cornish sea salt and freshly ground black pepper

Soak the beans in cold water to cover overnight. Drain the beans, rinse under cold running water and set aside. Heat a splash of rapeseed oil in a saucepan. Add the whole shallot, garlic cloves, carrot, celery, bay leaves and rosemary sprig and sweat for 2 minutes. Add the haricot beans, pour on enough water or fish stock to cover generously and bring to a simmer. Cover and simmer gently for 25 minutes or until tender. Discard the herbs and vegetables and season with salt and pepper to taste before serving.

Braised fennel

Serves 4

2 fennel bulbs

rapeseed oil for cooking

30g unsalted butter

75ml orange juice

Cornish sea salt and freshly ground black pepper

Remove the tough outer layer from the fennel. Halve the bulbs lengthways, then cut each half into 4 wedges, keeping the root intact so that the wedges don't fall apart. Heat a non-stick frying pan over a medium heat and add a drizzle of oil. Add the fennel wedges and cook for 2 minutes, turning once or twice, until starting to turn golden. Season with salt and pepper and add the butter and orange juice. Simmer for about 4 minutes until cooked. Check the seasoning before serving.

Braised lettuce

Serves 4

olive oil for cooking
50g unsalted butter
4 baby gem lettuces, halved
100ml orange juice
100ml roast fish stock (see page 222)
Cornish sea salt and freshly ground
black pepper

Heat a large non-stick frying pan over a medium heat, then add a drizzle of olive oil and the butter. Once bubbling, add the lettuces, cut side down, and season with salt and pepper. Cook for 2 minutes until the cut surfaces are starting to brown, then flip the lettuces over and colour for 2 minutes on the other side. Deglaze the pan with the orange juice and then add the fish stock. Bring to a simmer and cook for 5 minutes. Transfer the lettuces to a plate. Continue to simmer the liquid until reduced by half, then return the lettuces to the pan. Remove from the heat, spoon the reduced liquor over the lettuces and serve.

Deep-fried courgettes

Serves 4

4 courgettes
rapeseed oil for deep-frying
plain flour for dusting
Cornish sea salt and freshly ground
black pepper

Thinly slice the courgettes lengthways, then cut into matchsticks. Heat the oil in a deep-fryer or other heavy pan to 180°C. Put the flour in a large bowl and season well with salt and pepper. Add the courgettes and toss to coat, then remove, shaking off excess flour. Fry the courgettes in the hot oil, in batches as necessary, for 2 minutes until crispy. Remove and drain on kitchen paper. Season with a little salt and serve.

Barbecued vegetables

Serves 4

2 courgettes, sliced
2 red onions, peeled and quartered
500g button mushrooms, trimmed
2 red peppers, cored, deseeded and cut
into 2cm squares
olive oil to drizzle
2 tsp chopped thyme
1 tsp chopped garlic
Cornish sea salt and freshly ground
black pepper

Put all the vegetables into a large bowl, dividing the onions into petals as you add them. Season with salt and pepper, drizzle with olive oil and add the thyme and garlic. Using your hands, give the vegetables a good mix. Now thread them onto metal skewers, alternating the vegetables as you do so. When you are ready to barbecue the skewers, give them 4–5 minutes on each side.

Red wine shallots

Serves 10

4 large banana shallots, peeled
150ml red wine
75ml red wine vinegar
75g caster sugar
Cornish sea salt

Slice the shallots into fine rings and put into a clean container. Put the wine, wine vinegar and sugar into a saucepan and bring to a simmer over a medium heat. Add a pinch of salt. Pour the hot pickling liquor over the shallots, make sure they are submerged and leave to cool. Seal and leave for at least 12 hours before using. Stored in a sterilised jar in the fridge, these pickled shallots will keep for 3 months.

White wine shallots Finely chop the shallots, rather than slice into rings. Proceed as above, using white instead of red wine and wine vinegar.

Pickled onions

Serves 6

1kg silverskin onions, peeled and root
trimmed but intact

100ml dry white wine

100ml white wine vinegar

100g caster sugar

2 bay leaves

5 juniper berries

10 black peppercorns

Put all the ingredients into a saucepan and bring to
a simmer over a medium heat. Simmer for 1 minute,
then remove from the heat and allow to cool. Transfer
to a kilner jar or airtight container, seal and leave for at
least 24 hours, preferably a week before using. Stored in
a sterilised jar in the fridge, these pickled onions will be
good for 3 months.

Pickled baby onions in red wine Prepare 16 baby onions
as above, using red rather than white wine and red wine
vinegar. Omit the juniper berries.

Pickled grapes

Serves 4

40 grapes (red or green or a combination)

50ml white wine

50ml white wine vinegar

50ml water

50g caster sugar

pinch of sea salt

1 garlic clove, peeled and crushed

Wash the grapes, pat dry and put into a clean container.
Put the rest of the ingredients in a saucepan. Bring to
a simmer and simmer for 2 minutes, then pour over the
grapes, making sure they are covered. Allow to cool, then
seal and leave for at least 12 hours before using. Stored
in a sterilised jar in the fridge, these pickled grapes will
keep for 3 months.

Pickled mushrooms

Serves 8

2 shallots, peeled and finely chopped

150ml red wine vinegar

50ml light rapeseed oil

500g wild and/or cultivated mushrooms

Cornish sea salt and freshly ground
black pepper

Soak the shallots in the wine vinegar for 30 minutes. Heat
the oil in a large frying pan and pan-fry the mushrooms for
2 minutes until they begin to colour, seasoning with salt
and pepper. Add the shallots and wine vinegar, stirring to
deglaze, then remove from the heat. Stored in a jar in the
fridge, these mushrooms will keep for 2 weeks.

Pickled vegetables

Serves 4

1 fennel bulb, tough outer layer removed

2 banana shallots, peeled and finely sliced

2 carrots, peeled and finely sliced

2 celery sticks, de-stringed and sliced

1 thyme sprig

1 garlic clove, peeled and crushed

100ml white wine

100ml white wine vinegar

100ml water

100g caster sugar

Cornish sea salt and freshly ground
black pepper

Cut the fennel into wafer-thin slices with a mandolin,
ideally. Put in a large bowl with the rest of the vegetables,
thyme and garlic. Put the wine, wine vinegar, water and
sugar in a saucepan and bring to a simmer over a medium
heat, stirring. Simmer for 1 minute and then pour this
pickling liquor over the vegetables. Season with salt and
pepper. Transfer to a clean container, seal and leave for at
least 12 hours before serving. Stored in a sterilised jar in
the fridge, these pickled vegetables will keep for a month.

Spiced pickled vegetables Replace the fennel and thyme
with 1 thinly sliced red pepper, ½ red chilli, deseeded,
and 1 tsp fennel seeds. Discard the chilli before serving.

Tomato ketchup

Makes 400ml (enough for 10 servings)

olive oil for cooking

2 red onions, peeled and chopped

6 garlic cloves, peeled and sliced

20 black peppercorns

2.5kg ripe tomatoes, roughly chopped

100g caster sugar

4 tsp chopped thyme

1 cinnamon stick

4 bay leaves

300ml red wine vinegar

Cornish sea salt and freshly ground
black pepper

Heat a large saucepan over a medium heat and add a drizzle of olive oil. When hot, add the onions and garlic and cook for 2 minutes until the onions start to turn translucent. Meanwhile, tie the peppercorns in a piece of muslin. Add the tomatoes, sugar, thyme, cinnamon, bay leaves and peppercorn bundle to the pan and cook for 15 minutes until the tomatoes have broken down. Continue to cook until the tomato liquid has reduced right down, almost to nothing. Now add the wine vinegar and boil for 5 minutes. Remove the cinnamon, bay leaves and peppercorn bundle. Now transfer the contents of the pan to a blender or food processor and blend until smooth, then pass though a sieve into a bowl. Taste for seasoning, adding salt and pepper as required.

Transfer the ketchup to a clean container and allow to cool, then seal. It will keep in the fridge for up to a week; alternatively you can freeze it for up to a month.

Mushroom ketchup

Makes 200ml (enough for 6 servings)

olive oil for cooking

1 white onion, peeled and chopped

4 garlic cloves, peeled and finely
chopped

2 bay leaves

500g button mushrooms, finely sliced

100ml white wine

100ml white wine vinegar

500ml vegetable stock (see page 222)

50g soft brown sugar

Cornish sea salt and freshly ground
black pepper

Heat a large saucepan over a medium heat and add a drizzle of olive oil. Add the onion, garlic and bay leaves and sweat for 2 minutes. Add the mushrooms and cook until they are starting to colour and all the juices they release have evaporated and the pan is quite dry. Add the wine and let bubble until reduced by half, then add the wine vinegar and again reduce by half. Finally add the stock and sugar, stir to dissolve and simmer until the liquid has reduced right down, almost to nothing. Transfer the mixture to a blender and blend until smooth. Taste for seasoning, adding salt and pepper as required.

Transfer the ketchup to a clean container and allow to cool, then seal. It will keep in the fridge for up to a week; alternatively you can freeze it for up to a month.

Breads

Fermented 'starter dough'

Makes enough for 4 loaves

160ml fermented peach or pear juice
(see method)

280g white bread flour

15g fresh yeast

I use this 'starter dough' for most of my breads. It lends an incredible depth of flavour.

To create the fermented fruit juice, a couple of days before making your bread, open a 400g tin of peaches or pears. Tip into a bowl, cover and leave to ferment for 2 days. Once fermented, transfer the fruit and juice to a blender and blitz to a smooth liquid, then pass through a sieve into a jug.

Put the flour, yeast and fermented juice into an electric mixer fitted with a dough hook and mix on a high speed until a smooth dough has formed. Transfer to a lidded container. The fermented 'starter' dough will live in the fridge happily for up to 5 days… but keep an eye on it as it might try to escape!

White bread

Makes 1 loaf or 5–10 rolls (depending on size)

250g white bread flour

60g fermented 'starter' dough
(see above)

150ml water

15g fresh yeast

15g unsalted butter

10g fine sea salt

Put all the ingredients, except the salt, into an electric mixer fitted with a dough hook and mix on a high speed for 6 minutes. Add the salt and mix for another 2 minutes. Transfer the dough to a floured bowl, cover with a damp cloth and leave in a warm place to rise for 30 minutes. On a floured surface, knock back the risen dough. The dough is now ready to shape, either into loaves or rolls.

To shape and bake a loaf Shape into a round or other loaf shape and place on a baking sheet, or form into an oblong and place in a standard 500g loaf tin. Cover with a damp cloth and leave to prove in a warm place until doubled in size, about 40 minutes. Meanwhile, heat the oven to 220°C/Gas 7.

Sprinkle the loaf with flour. Bake for 20 minutes or until golden brown and the loaf sounds hollow when tapped on the underside. Transfer to a wire rack and leave to cool before serving.

To shape and bake rolls Divide the bread dough into 50g balls (or 100g balls for burger-size rolls). The best way to do this is to use electric scales. On a floured surface, take a portion of dough and using both hands and fingertips, bring the dough from the bottom to the top and turn the dough over. Now, using the sides of both hands, roll the dough in a circle until you have a smooth round roll. Repeat to shape the rest. Place on a floured baking tray, cover with a damp cloth and leave to prove in a warm place until doubled in size, about 40 minutes. Meanwhile, heat the oven to 220°C/Gas 7.

Sprinkle the rolls with flour. Bake for 12–15 minutes or until golden brown. Cool on a wire rack before serving.

Fennel seed bread Add 20g toasted fennel seeds to the dough with the salt. Let rise, shape and prove as for white bread. Sprinkle fennel seeds over the surface of the loaf or rolls and dust with flour before baking.

Poppy and sesame seed bread Add 30g each poppy and sesame seeds to the dough with the salt. Let rise, shape and prove as for white bread. Sprinkle poppy and sesame seeds over the surface of the loaf or rolls and dust with a little flour before baking.

Granary bread

Makes 1 loaf or 6–12 rolls (depending on size)

100g white bread flour

200g granary bread flour

60g fermented 'starter' dough (see left)

160ml water

15g fresh yeast

15g unsalted butter

10g fine sea salt

Put all the ingredients, except the salt, into an electric mixer fitted with a dough hook and mix on a high speed for 6 minutes. Add the salt and mix for another 2 minutes. Transfer the dough to a floured bowl, cover with a damp cloth and leave in a warm place to rise for 30 minutes.

On a floured surface, knock back the risen dough. It is now ready to shape, either into loaves or rolls (see left). Cover with a damp cloth and leave to prove in a warm place until doubled in size, about 40 minutes. Meanwhile, heat the oven to 220°C/Gas 7.

Sprinkle the surface of the bread with flour. Bake for 15–20 minutes or until golden brown and the bread sounds hollow when tapped on the underside. Transfer to a wire rack and leave to cool before serving.

Cider bread Make the dough as above, replacing the water with 150ml medium-dry cider. Leave to rise, shape, prove and bake as above.

Treacle bread

Makes 2 loaves

250g white bread flour

250g granary bread flour

200ml water

30g fresh yeast

30g unsalted butter

100g black treacle

15g fine sea salt

Put all the ingredients, except the salt, into an electric mixer fitted with a dough hook and mix on a high speed for 6 minutes. Add the salt and mix for another 2 minutes.

Transfer the dough to a floured bowl, cover with a damp cloth and leave in a warm place to rise for 30 minutes.

On a floured surface, knock back the risen dough. Divide in half and shape each piece into a loaf (see left). Cover with a damp cloth and leave to prove in a warm place until doubled in size, about 40 minutes. Meanwhile, heat the oven to 220°C/Gas 7.

Sprinkle the loaf with flour. Bake for 20 minutes or until golden brown and the loaf sounds hollow when tapped on the underside. Transfer to a wire rack and leave to cool before serving.

Tarragon brioche

Makes 3 loaves

500g white bread flour

20g fresh yeast

50g caster sugar

5 eggs

2 tbsp chopped tarragon

2 tsp fine sea salt

250g unsalted butter, softened

Put the flour, yeast, sugar and eggs into an electric mixer fitted with a dough hook and mix on a medium speed for 6 minutes. Add the tarragon and salt. Now slowly add the butter, a little at a time, continuing to mix until it is all incorporated. Remove the bowl from the machine and cover with a damp cloth. Leave the dough to prove in a warm place for 1 hour.

On a floured surface, knock back the risen dough and divide into 3 equal pieces. Grease 3 standard 500g loaf tins and place the dough in the tins. Cover with a damp cloth and leave to prove in a warm place for 1 hour. Meanwhile, heat the oven to 200°C/Gas 6.

Slide the loaf tins into the oven and bake for 20 minutes or until golden brown. Remove the brioche from the oven and place on a wire rack to cool. Eat the same day or freeze for up to a month.

Preparation techniques

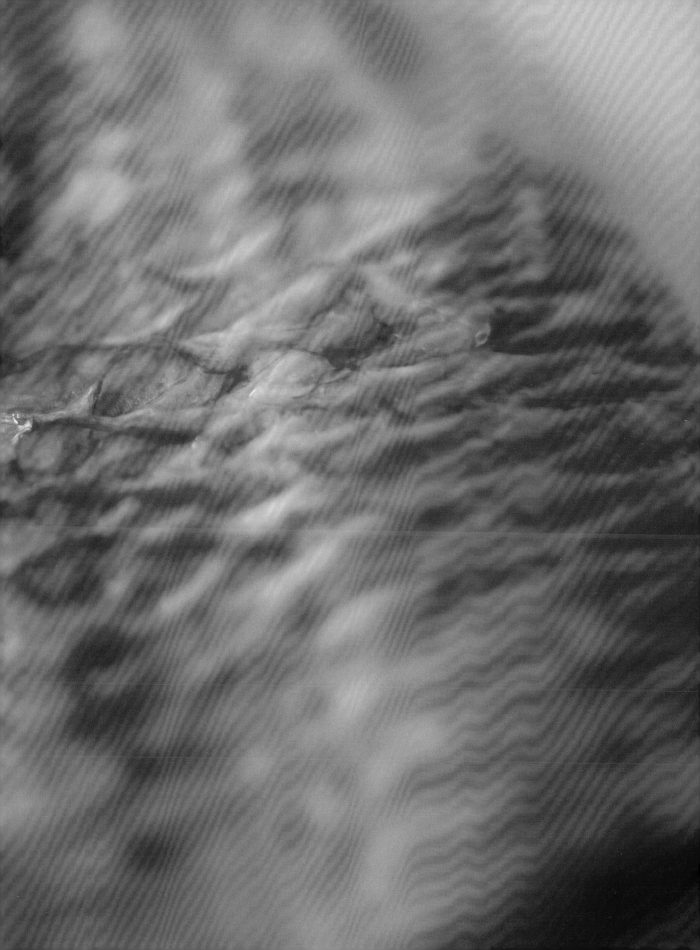

Flat fish

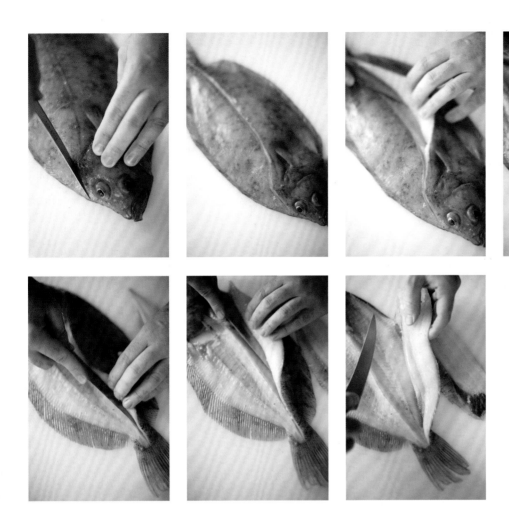

Filleting a flat fish

A flat fish yields four fillets and has two distinct sides. The top side displays the species' individual characteristics – the orange spots of a plaice, or the lumpy skin of a turbot, for example. The underside should be a clean, creamy white. Make sure the fish has been gutted and is as dry as possible. Unless you've caught the fish yourself, it will most likely be gutted. If not, it's straightforward to do (see page 241).

Before you start filleting, make sure your chopping board is secure by placing a damp cloth underneath it to stop it slipping. A razor-sharp knife is equally important; a blunt knife will slip and is therefore dangerous. Lay the fish on the chopping board with the head pointing away from you. Insert your knife at the side of the head and bring it around to the centre of the neck. Now run the knife down the centre bone to the end of the tail, in one straight line. Then, starting from the cut at the bottom of the head, carefully cut the fillet free from the skeleton, holding the knife flat against the bones and working towards the edge of the fish. When you have freed all the flesh from the bone, cut through the skin at the tail end and work up the edge of the fish until you reach the top where you originally started. You should now have released the first fillet.

To remove the second fillet, turn the fish around so the head is pointing towards you. Starting from the tail and working up, do exactly the same as before until the fillet is released. Flip the fish over and repeat on the other side to release the other two fillets.

Skinning a flat fish fillet
Make sure your chopping board is secure and your knife is sharp. Lay the fillet skin side down on the board and trim away the skirt from the outer edge. (You'll find it much easier to skin the fillet if you do this first.)

Now, holding the tail end down with one hand, slightly angle your knife down towards the board. Using the length of the knife and cutting smoothly, run the knife along the skin to release the fillet from it. The aim is to leave as little flesh on the skin as possible, if any! Sometimes little bits of skin are left on the flesh, but you can just trim these away carefully.

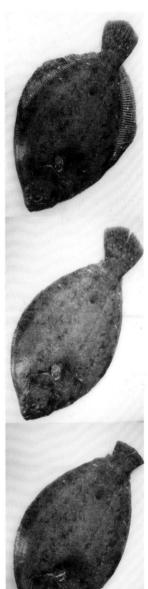

Preparing a flat fish to cook whole

First make sure the fish has been gutted and is free from scales and sea slime. If the guts are still in place you'll find them easy to remove. They are situated just below the head and pectoral fin, so feel around with your fingers until you locate the soft innards. Make a semi-circular around the edge of the gut cavity, insert your fingers and pull the guts out. Rinse the cavity.

Now, using strong scissors, trim away the skirt from around the edge of the fish. Cut off all the fins and trim the tail. On bigger fish like turbot you may want to remove the gills and skin, but I don't bother. I know I'm not going to eat the gills, so they don't offend me and I like to keep the skin on because it gives the fish some protection during cooking.

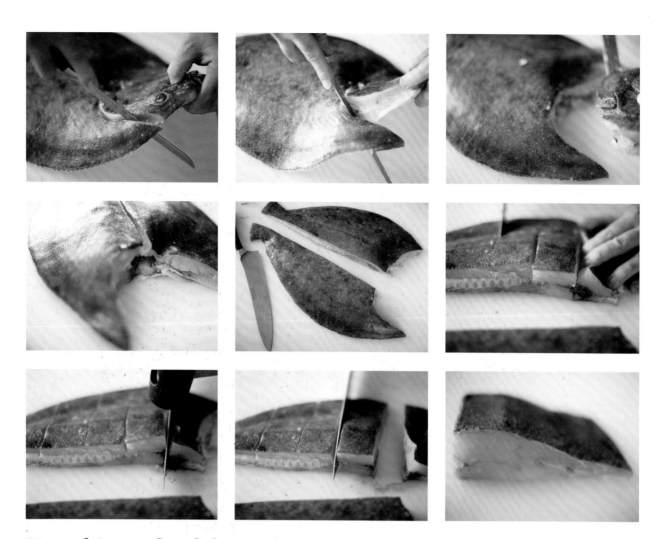

Tranching a flat fish

This is the best way to cook a big flat fish. You will need a sharp large cook's knife, scissors and a rubber mallet or old rolling pin that you don't mind getting dented.

Lay the fish on a chopping board. Remove the skirt and fins (see page 241), then cut around the head and remove it. Using the cook's knife, make a slice along the central bone from the head to the tail. The aim is to cut through this bone, so try to get the knife as central as possible. Use the mallet to give the knife a firm tap and it should go through the bone, leaving you two clean sides of fish.

Next, turn the sides around and mark out the size of portion you want, slicing down to the bone at the point where you want to cut it. Obviously, you will need to adjust the intervals of your cuts, making them wider towards the tail end, to give roughly equal-sized portions.

Again hold the knife firmly against the exposed bone and hit hard with the mallet to give you a clean quick cut. You now have a tranche ready for cooking. Repeat to cut the rest of your tranches.

Tranching is only suitable for bigger flat fish, such as turbot and brill, which yield fairly chunky portions.

Round fish

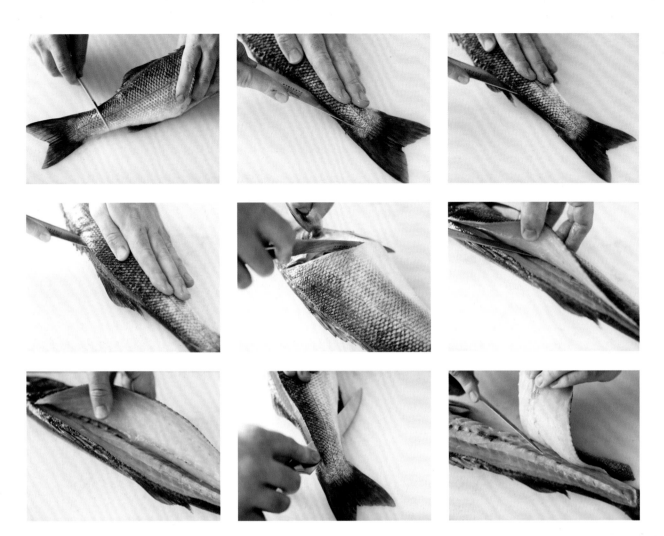

Descaling

If you plan on eating your fish with the skin on – which is deliciously crisp after grilling, frying or roasting – you will want to descale it. Most of the fish you buy will have been descaled already, or your fishmonger will offer to do it for you, but should you need to descale it yourself, it really isn't difficult. It's easiest to descale a fish when whole and to do so underwater, as this stops the scales from flying all over your kitchen.

Fill your sink with enough water to cover the fish. Now, holding the fish by the tail, submerge it in the water. Using a descaler or the back of a knife, push firmly against the skin from the tail to the head (ie in the opposite direction to the way the scales lie) and the scales will come off. Make sure you are careful not to push too hard as this will crush the flesh. Turn the fish over and repeat on the other side. When all the scales are off, wash and dry the fish, checking for any stray scales. It is then ready to use.

Filleting a round fish

A round fish yields two fillets. Make sure the fish has been descaled and gutted, and that all the fins and scales have been removed (see page 248). Use a large chopping board and make sure it is firmly secure on your worktop by placing a damp cloth underneath it, and that your knife is very sharp.

Lay the fish on the board with the belly facing away from you. Make a cut at the tail end and bring the knife up along the fish, just above the backbone to the head (this cut only needs to be a few centimetres deep). When you reach the head end, cut across the fish diagonally just behind the gills, just as far as the skeleton. Now, in a firm, sweeping motion, work the knife flat across the bones from the tail to the head end, to ease the fillet away. Cut through the flesh at the tail end to release the fillet and carefully work it away from the rib cage.

continued on next page

To remove the second fillet you need to flip the fish over and follow the same procedure, but working from the head down to the tail. So, start by making an incision at the head end and make a shallow cut along the backbone, just above it, down to the tail.

Now carefully skim the knife over the skeleton, working smoothly from head to tail. Cut through the fillet at the head end to release the fillet and carefully work it away from the rib cage until it is free. You will now have two fillets and a clean skeleton.

PREPARATION TECHNIQUES

Skinning a fillet

To skin the fillet make sure your board is secure and your knife is sharp. Lay the fillet in front of you and trim the outer edge to neaten. Now, firmly holding the skin at the tail end with one hand, slightly angle your knife down towards the board, so that when you cut into the fillet the knife will run along the skin and won't cut into the fish. Use the length of your knife as you move the knife over the skin to release the fillet from it, and avoid being aggressive with your movements. Sometimes little bits of skin get left on the fillet; just trim these off carefully.

Pin-boning

Pin bones are not something that you want to get stuck in your throat, so it's always best to remove them and very easy to do so. Lay the fish fillet on your chopping board, flesh side up. Using your fingers as a guide, feel along the centre of the fillet for any small bones. With a pair of strong tweezers, grab hold of any pin bone you find and pull firmly – towards the end where the head would have been – to remove it.

Preparing a round fish to cook whole

To gut the fish, if necessary, hold it belly side up in one hand with the head pointing away from you. Insert the tip of the knife at the anal vent and make a shallow cut through the flesh along the belly and up to the throat to open up the cavity. Using your hand, pull out all the guts from inside. You really do need to take care as you do this, as there may be sharp hooks and/or little spiny fish caught inside. Rinse the cavity well. Now, using strong scissors, remove all the fins and trim the tail. Cut out the gills, too. Leave the skin in place to protect the fish during cooking.

Steaking a round fish

Certain round fish really benefit from being cooked on the bone as steaks, because it seems to keep the texture firm and the fish moist – great for braising in a stew, for example.

Using a very sharp knife, mark the fish where you want to portion it, then slice straight through, using a mallet to force the knife through the bone if necessary. Make sure that the portions are equal or they won't cook evenly.

Butterflying fish

This is a great technique for smaller round fish, such as sardines, herring and small red mullet. If necessary, remove the guts (see page 248) and cut off the head, fins and gills. Extend the cut from gutting the fish so the fish is opened from top to tail end.

Now cut down both sides of the skeleton to release the flesh, without cutting right through. Using the palm of your hand, gently push down onto the back of the fish until the backbone is flat against the chopping board and the fillets are either side.

With most fish, you can simply pull out the backbone with your fingers, but if that isn't possible, use strong scissors and then trim off the backbone. Now use a filleting knife to trim the fish neatly and pin-bone using tweezers (see page 247). The butterflied fish is now ready to cook.

Filleting rays and skate

These fish have cartilage rather than bones and can simply be filleted to give lovely bone-free fillets. Skinning ray is quite difficult, so when you buy a ray wing, always buy it skinned.

Lay the ray wing on your chopping board and, using a serrated knife, trim off the thick cartilage that attached the wing to the body. Trim off any sinew and membrane left behind from skinning too.

Now, using a sharp filleting knife and working from the triangular point of the wing to the edge, cut the first fillet free from the cartilagineous framework by skimming the knife smoothly over the framework, keeping it as close to the cartilage as possible.

To remove the second fillet, turn the wing over, so the cartilage is flat against the board, and repeat the procedure. Your two ray or skate fillets are now ready to cook.

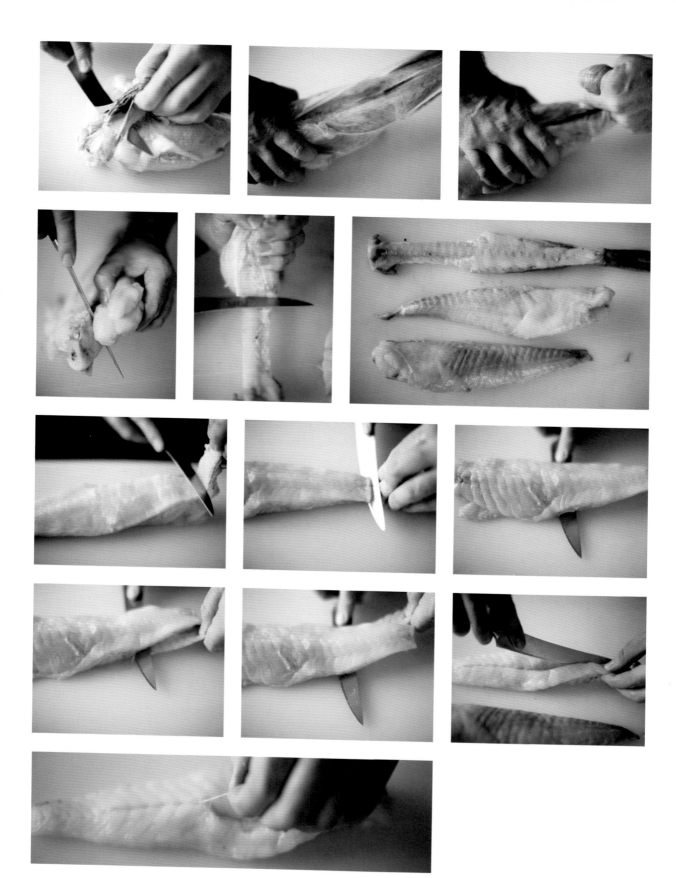

PREPARATION TECHNIQUES

Preparing monkfish Filleting

monkfish is easier than other fish because it has only one central bone that runs along its entire length, but first you need to remove the skin. Take your monkfish tail and release the skin at the head end with your knife. Grasp this skin and pull towards the tail end with some force to remove the skin in one piece.

Now to fillet the monkfish, take a sharp knife and run it along one side of the bone, leaving no flesh behind on the bone. Repeat on the other side of the bone. You now have your two monkfish fillets.

Monkfish also has an inedible outer membrane that must be removed. As if you were skinning the fillet, grab a small bit of flesh at the tail end and cut into it. Now, holding the tail end with one hand, bring the knife from the tail to the thick end, removing as much of the membrane as possible.

Flip the fillet over and you'll expose the thin sinew in the red bloodline running along the fillet. Using the tip of your knife, cut this out. Trim off any remaining membrane. Your fish is now ready to cook.

Shellfish

Cooking lobster

It is possible to kill a live lobster by plunging a knife into the cross on its head and splitting it lengthways quickly in two, but in reality it is quite hard to kill it with one blow. Instead I prefer to boil this crustacean alive but calmed. The lobster may be a simple creature, with a long nerve cord rather than a brain, but it still deserves to be treated humanely.

Before boiling, I put the lobster in the freezer for about 30 minutes until it's calmed to the point of hardly moving. Then I have a big pan of fast-boiling salted water ready.

To cook the lobster, take it from the freezer and firmly insert the tip of a strong knife into the cross on the head to kill it instantly, then plunge it straight into the boiling water. Bring back to the boil. From this point, I allow 10 minutes for a lobster weighing 700g and add 1 minute for every 100g above that. For a smaller 500–600g lobster, I allow 8 minutes. When the cooking time is up, lift out the lobster and place it on a tray to cool.

Preparing lobster

When the lobster is cool enough to handle, you can extract the meat. Lay it on your chopping board and split it in half lengthways from head to tail, using a large, heavy knife. Remove the small stomach sac in the head and the dark intestinal tract that runs along the length of the tail. Don't discard the liver or 'tomalley', which is delicious. The red coral in female lobsters is good to eat too. Tap the claws firmly with the back of a heavy knife to crack them open and release the meat. You can also pull out the meat from the thin legs.

Cooking crab

I put crabs into the freezer an hour or so before cooking to calm them down. Also, I always try to cook my crabs in sea water, but you can use 50g salt to 1 litre tap water. Bring your salty water to a fast boil. Take the crab from the freezer and plunge an awl or other sharp pointed tool into one of the two points on its underside to kill it instantly, then plunge it into the boiling water. Once the water comes back to the boil, cook for 15 minutes if the crab is 600g or less, adding 2 minutes for every extra 100g. As soon as the crab is cooked, lift it out onto a tray to cool.

Preparing crab

Remove all the legs and claws from the cooked crab, by twisting them away from the body. Now, holding the crab in both hands, use your thumbs to push the body up and out of the hard top shell. Remove the dead man's fingers, stomach sac and hard membranes from the body shell. Using a spoon, remove the brown crab from the top shell and put it into a bowl. Now cut the body in half with a sharp knife to reveal all the little channels of white crab meat. Use a crab pick or the back of a spoon to pick out all the crab meat from these crevices and put it into a bowl. Then, with a heavy knife, break the claw with one hard tap if possible and pick out the crab meat, removing the cartilage in the middle of each claw. Do the same to extract the meat from the legs. When you have taken out all the crab meat, go through it carefully with your fingers a couple of times to check for any stray fragments of shell.

Opening oysters

I find an oyster knife isn't the best implement for shucking an oyster unless you've one with a small blade; I prefer a sturdy butter-knife-sized knife.

Hold the oyster flat side up in a folded tea towel (for protection), in one hand. Insert the knife into the hinge of the oyster and wiggle at the hinge, using a little force, until you hear a popping sound and it yields. Run the knife along the roof of the flat side to cut the attaching muscle and release the oyster from the top shell. Using the same knife, carefully cut away the same muscle from the bottom shell and flip the oyster over in the shell, being careful to retain all the juices. The oyster is now ready.

PREPARATION TECHNIQUES

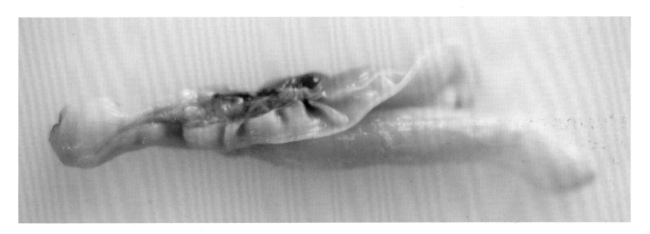

  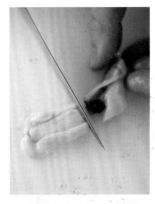 

Preparing razor clams

These tasty bivalves must always be live when cooked. Rinse well, then steam them open in a covered pan with a little white wine or water. Allow to cool slightly before pulling the clams from their shells. Now, to prepare them, cut the longer part of the clam away from the dark sac. Then cut off the rounder end, the other side of the sac. Remove the wing-like covering from the body and scrape off any sand. You can now slice both of these parts into small slices or keep them whole. Discard the dark sac.

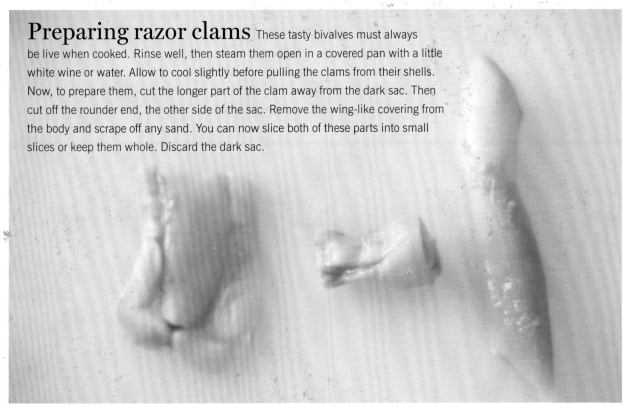

PREPARATION TECHNIQUES

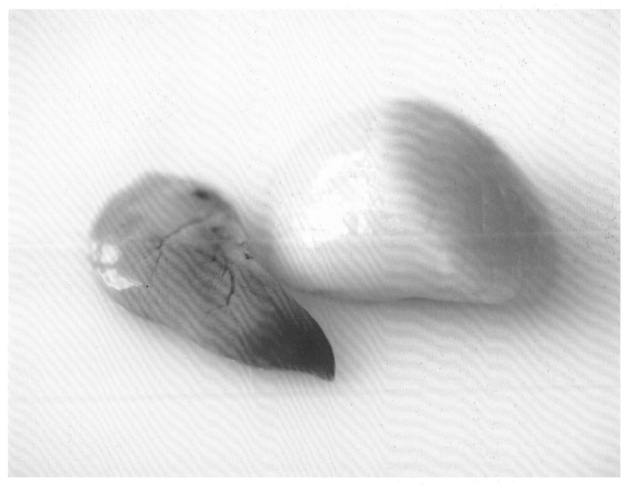

Opening scallops

This is a fun task once you get the hang of it. Make sure your scallops are alive – either tightly shut or ready to close when firmly tapped.

To open, hold the scallop firmly between the fingers and thumb of one hand, so the flatter side of the scallop shell is facing upwards. Insert the tip of a strong, fairly small knife between the shells at the corner of the hinge and twist to break it. Now bring the knife down between the shells to separate them and pull off the top shell. Using a thin, flat spoon, scrape around the scallop and the other bits until you release everything from the shell. Then grab the scallop, roe and skirt with your hands and find the white muscle. Use your thumb and forefinger to release the scallop meat from the muscle. Now work around the scallop, carefully removing the very thin membrane until you have in your hand just the white scallop meat. The plump, bright orange coral, which comes away with the muscle, can be cut free and cooked with the white scallop.

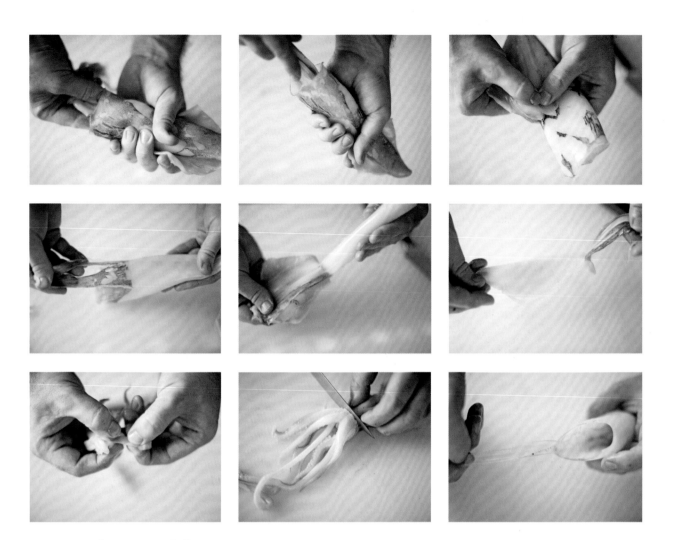

Preparing squid
Make sure your squid is clean and white, with no pink tinges. Holding the body in one hand, grab the head and pull it firmly and carefully – the innards that are attached to it will come away with it. If the squid hasn't released its ink already, you'll find the ink sac within the innards.

Pull the fins or 'wings' away from the sides of the body. Now remove the purplish skin covering the body. Carefully scrape the body and fins with your knife to remove any ink or excess skin and give the fins a quick rinse.

Returning to the head, take hold of the tentacles and squeeze the head to remove the sharp beak, pulling it out. Using a sharp knife, cut the tentacles away from the head, just under the eyes. Rinse the tentacles.

Finally, pull out the plastic-looking quill from the body and any other insides that look as though they shouldn't be there. Give the body a quick rinse. At this point you can cut the squid body open or slice it into rings. The fins can also be cut into smaller pieces. Cook the body, fins and tentacles as required.

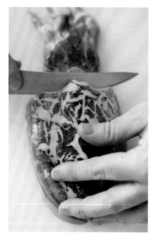   

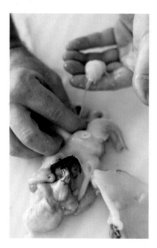 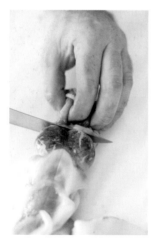  

Preparing cuttlefish
Using a knife, cut through the hard part at the base of the head to release the cuttlebone. With your fingers, carefully push out the cuttlebone (akin to the squid's transparent quill).

Separate the head and tentacles from the body, pulling the head firmly (as you would for squid but expect more of the innards to remain inside the body). Now carefully reach inside the body with your hand to release the innards, taking care to avoid rupturing the ink sac if it is still intact, otherwise you'll end up in a mess!

Returning to the head, squeeze out the beak and cut off the tentacles at the eyes. Finally peel off the skin from the body – you'll find this quite easy to do.

Cuttlefish can be cooked in the same way as squid, but I much prefer to braise them slowly to tenderise their thicker, tougher flesh.

Index

Acknowledgements

The summer of 2011 wasn't a fun one for Rachel, my wife, as she spent most of it on her own and looking after the kids while I was writing this book! Thank you Rachel, for your patience, support and love, as always. Jacob and Jessica, thanks for looking after Mummy and I hope you will forgive me for all the missed opportunities at the beach. Not forgetting Bud, my lurcher, for being happy to see me at any time of the day or night.

To Mum and Dad, thank you for your inspiration and for giving me the work ethic and motivation to write a book about the subject I love best… food. To Ashley – I've only got one brother. And to the rest of the family – I hope you like the book and I'm sure some of the stories and experiences in it involved you.

To Peter Biggs, thanks for all the hard work and stolen prep and ideas for the book and photos. To Steffi, Charlotte and Damon, thank you for everything and sorry for making the restaurant such a mess during the photo shoots and writing sessions. To Ian, for your continued dedication and loyalty. To Danny for your loyalty and telling it like it is… and for keeping all the fish prepped. And to my chefs: Chris (Hotpot) Simpson, Deano, Tim (Christian) Barnes, Redas Katauskas (the finest 'Cornish' chef I know), Thomas Carr, Dennis 'The Menace' Easton, Simon Davies, Andrew Snell, Georgie Dent and Henry Culverhouse. And to my front of house: Emma Jane (EM-J) Howman, Anna Davey and Daniel Southern. Thanks also to the staff at St Enodoc Hotel: Kate Simms, Jane Walkey, Sarah Graham and Gail George. Without my team I couldn't do anything.

A big thank you to Kim and Tina Oxenham for all their help and support since returning to Rock. Thanks also to Tim Alsop for getting all the fish for the book in prime condition, David Griffen for his help at the beginning of the project, Paul 'Geezer' Ripley for being there and employing me at The Seafood, Mitch Tonks for advice and inspiration, David Hunter for helping with all things moneywise, Darren Smith for always being there if I need him, and Karen de Salis for the continuous flow of tea and coffee.

To all at Quadrille, including Anne Furniss for believing in me and letting me write the book I wanted to write, Helen Lewis for making the book look the bees knees and Clare Lattin for promoting it. To Lawrence Morton for your fantastic design and Janet Illsley for organising my ideas so that they make sense and for putting up with me missing deadlines. Finally, to David Loftus, the fastest shot in the Southwest!

And last but not least to Rick Stein for writing the foreword and making me prep fish for a whole year in the early days!

Editorial director Anne Furniss
Creative director Helen Lewis
Project editor Janet Illsley
Designer Lawrence Morton
Photographer David Loftus
Food for photography Nathan Outlaw
Production Leonie Kellman, Vincent Smith

First published in 2012 by Quadrille Publishing Limited Alhambra House, 27–31 Charing Cross Road, London WC2H 0LS www.quadrille.co.uk

10 9 8 7 6 5 4 3 2

Text © 2012 Nathan Outlaw
Photography © 2012 David Loftus
Jacket illustration © 2012 Tim Hopgood
Design and layout © 2012 Quadrille Publishing Limited

Cataloguing in Publication Data: a catalogue record for this book is available from the British Library.

978 184949 115 0

Printed in China